Frommer's®

# Sydney
## day BY day®

### 2nd Edition

## by Lee Atkinson

WILEY

John Wiley & Sons, Inc.

# Contents

Published by:

# John Wiley & Sons, Inc.

111 River St.
Hoboken, NJ 07030-5774

Copyright © 2012 John Wiley & Sons, Inc., Hoboken, New Jersey. All rights reserved. No part of this publication may be reproduced, stored in a retrieval system or transmitted in any form or by any means, electronic, mechanical, photocopying, recording, scanning or otherwise, except as permitted under Sections 107 or 108 of the 1976 United States Copyright Act, without either the prior written permission of the Publisher, or authorization through payment of the appropriate per-copy fee to the Copyright Clearance Center, 222 Rosewood Drive, Danvers, MA 01923, 978/750-8400, fax 978/646-8600. Requests to the Publisher for permission should be addressed to the Permissions Department, John Wiley & Sons, Inc., 111 River Street, Hoboken, NJ 07030, 201/748-6011, fax 201/748-6008, or online at http://www.wiley.com/go/permissions.

Wiley and the Wiley logo are trademarks or registered trademarks of John Wiley & Sons, Inc. Frommer's is a trademark or registered trademark of Arthur Frommer. Used under license. All other trademarks are the property of their respective owners. John Wiley & Sons, Inc. is not associated with any product or vendor mentioned in this book.

ISBN 978-1-118-30480-8 (paper); ISBN 978-1-118-33529-1(ebk); ISBN 978-1-118-33417-1 (ebk); ISBN 978-1-118-33193-4 (ebk)

Editor: Alexia Travaglini
Production Editor: Heather Wilcox
Photo Editor: Richard Fox
Cartographer: Roberta Stockwell
Production by Wiley Indianapolis Composition Services

For information on our other products and services or to obtain technical support, please contact our Customer Care Department within the U.S. at 877/762-2974, outside the U.S. at 317/572-3993 or fax 317/572-4002.

Wiley also publishes its books in a variety of electronic formats. Some content that appears in print may not be available in electronic formats.

Manufactured in China

5  4  3  2  1

# A Note from the Editorial Director

Organizing your time. That's what this guide is all about.

Other guides give you long lists of things to see and do and then expect you to fit the pieces together. The Day by Day guides are different. These guides tell you the best of everything, and then they show you how to see it *in the smartest, most time-efficient way*. Our authors have designed detailed itineraries organized by time, neighborhood, or special interest. And each tour comes with a bulleted map that takes you from stop to stop.

Hoping to tour the highlights of Sydney Harbour or sample the city's multicultural fare? Planning a trip to Bondi Beach or a shopping trip on Oxford Street? Whatever your interest or schedule, the Day by Days give you the smartest routes to follow. Not only do we take you to the top attractions, hotels, and restaurants, but we also help you access those special moments that locals get to experience—those "finds" that turn tourists into travelers.

The Day by Days are also your top choice if you're looking for one complete guide for all your travel needs. The best hotels and restaurants for every budget, the greatest shopping values, the wildest nightlife—it's all here.

Why should you trust our judgment? Because our authors personally visit each place they write about. They're an independent lot who say what they think and would never include places they wouldn't recommend to their best friends. They're also open to suggestions from readers. If you'd like to contact them, please send your comments our way at feedback@frommers.com, and we'll pass them on.

Enjoy your Day by Day guide—the most helpful travel companion you can buy. And have the trip of a lifetime.

Warm regards,

Kelly Regan, Editorial Director
Frommer's Travel Guides

# About the Author

**Lee Atkinson** is a freelance travel writer and guidebook author based in Australia. Her stories regularly appear in the travel sections of various newspapers and glossy travel magazines in Australia and throughout the world. She is the author of eight travel books, including *Frommer's Australia* (co-author), *Frommer's Sydney Free & Dirt Cheap*, *Frommer's Tasmania Day by Day*, and *Frommer's Bali Day by Day*.

# Advisory & Disclaimer

Travel information can change quickly and unexpectedly, and we strongly advise you to confirm important details locally before traveling, including information on visas, health and safety, traffic and transport, hotels, shopping, and eating out. We also encourage you to stay alert while traveling and to remain aware of your surroundings. Avoid civil disturbances, and keep a close eye on cameras, purses, wallets, and other valuables.

While we have endeavored to ensure that the information contained within this guide is accurate and up-to-date at the time of publication, we make no representations or warranties with respect to the accuracy or completeness of the contents of this work and specifically disclaim all warranties, including without limitation warranties of fitness for a particular purpose. We accept no responsibility or liability for any inaccuracy or errors or omissions, or for any inconvenience, loss, damage, costs, or expenses of any nature whatsoever incurred or suffered by anyone as a result of any advice or information contained in this guide.

The inclusion of a company, organization, or website in this guide as a service provider and/or potential source of further information does not mean that we endorse them or the information they provide. Be aware that information provided through some websites may be unreliable and can change without notice. Neither the publisher nor author shall be liable for any damages arising herefrom.

# Star Ratings, Icons & Abbreviations

Every hotel, restaurant, and attraction listing in this guide has been ranked for quality, value, service, amenities, and special features using a **star-rating system.** Hotels, restaurants, attractions, shopping, and nightlife are rated on a scale of zero stars (recommended) to three stars (exceptional). In addition to the star-rating system, we also use a **kids icon** to point out the best bets for families. Within each tour, we recommend cafes, bars, or restaurants where you can take a break. Each of these stops appears in a shaded box marked with a coffee-cup-shaped bullet ☕.

The following **abbreviations** are used for credit cards:

| | | | | | |
|---|---|---|---|---|---|
| AE | American Express | DISC | Discover | V | Visa |
| DC | Diners Club | MC | MasterCard | | |

# Travel Resources at Frommers.com

Frommer's travel resources don't end with this guide. Frommer's website, **www.frommers.com,** has travel information on more than 4,000 destinations. We update features regularly, giving you access to the most current trip-planning information and the best airfare, lodging, and car-rental bargains. You can also listen to podcasts, connect with other Frommers.com members through our active-reader forums, share your travel photos, read blogs from guidebook editors and fellow travelers, and much more.

# A Note on Prices

In the "Take a Break" and "Best Bets" sections of this book, we have used a system of dollar signs to show a range of costs for 1 night in a hotel (the price of a double-occupancy room) or the cost of an entree at a restaurant. Use the following table to decipher the dollar signs:

| Cost | Hotels | Restaurants |
|------|--------|-------------|
| $ | under $100 | under $10 |
| $$ | $100–$200 | $10–$20 |
| $$$ | $200–$300 | $20–$30 |
| $$$$ | $300–$400 | $30–$40 |
| $$$$$ | over $400 | over $40 |

# An Invitation to the Reader

In researching this book, we discovered many wonderful places—hotels, restaurants, shops, and more. We're sure you'll find others. Please tell us about them, so we can share the information with your fellow travelers in upcoming editions. If you were disappointed with a recommendation, we'd love to know that, too. Please write to:

*Frommer's Sydney Day by Day,* 2nd Edition
John Wiley & Sons, Inc. • 111 River St. • Hoboken, NJ 07030-5774

# 15 Favorite
## Moments

# 15 Favorite **Moments**

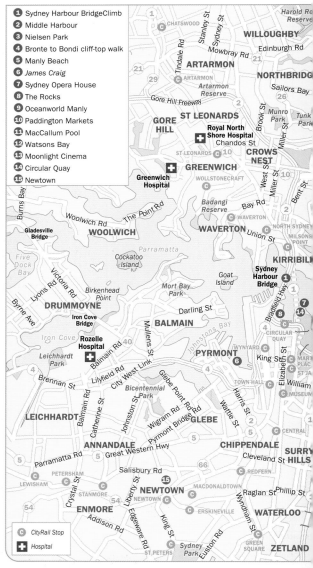

*Previous page: The beachfront park at Watson's Bay is a very popular spot for families and day trippers on the harbor ferry, especially for weekend picnics.*

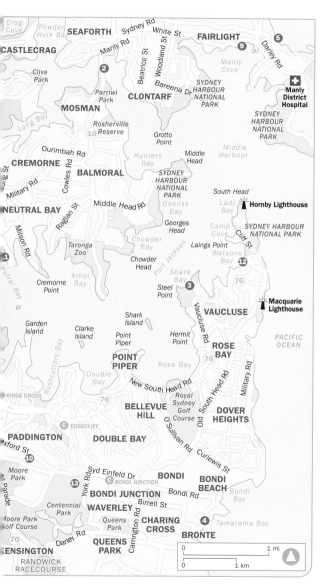

When it comes to having a good time in Sydney, chances are you're on, in, or near the water. Sydney's spectacular harbor, one of the biggest on the planet, is not only one of the world's most beautiful waterways, it's also the spiritual, historical, and cultural heart of the city. The focus of almost all of the city's celebrations, the waterfront is where we prefer to be, whether it's sailing on a summer afternoon, stepping out on a waterside bushwalk, picnicking in a sheltered cove, or gazing at the fabulous scenery, wishing we could afford one of those big houses with a million-dollar view. If we're not on or beside Sydney Harbour, we're at the beach. Here are 15 special things to do in Sydney.

**❶ Getting a bird's-eye view of Sydney from the top of the Coathanger on a Sydney Harbour BridgeClimb.** It's a long way to the top, and you'll need a head for heights, but the view is guaranteed to take your breath away. Best time is just at sunset, when you can watch the city light up. *See p 11.*

**❷ Exploring Sydney Harbour at sea level on a guided kayaking tour.** Get away from the tourist throng and discover the real Sydney as you paddle around the sheltered bays of Middle Harbour and poke around the deep water frontages of the city's rich and famous. It's a view of Sydney that few people get. *See p 25.*

**❸ Unpacking a picnic at one of the harborside parks and watching the world sail by.** This is the

*Kayak tour near Spit Bridge in Middle Harbour.*

thing to do any summer Sunday. With more than 240km (149 miles) of foreshore and dozens of parks to choose from, my pick is Nielsen Park with its sheltered, shark-free beach. *See p 33.*

**❹ Watching the sun rise out of the sea on the Bronte to Bondi cliff-top walk followed by a beachside breakfast.** If you can't face an early start, go at sunset and finish with a cocktail by the beach at Ravesi's Hotel in Bondi. *See p 31.*

**❺ Cruising between the heads on the Manly Ferry, followed by a promenade along The Corso, or a surfing lesson at Manly Beach.** At around $7 each way the half-hour trip is one of the best value cruises in the world. And once you get there, it's just like the 1940s slogan says: "Seven miles from Sydney, and a thousand miles from care." *See p 19.*

**❻ Learning the ropes aboard the tall ship *James Craig*.** Anywhere else in the world and this 19th-century, three-masted iron bark would be collecting dust in a museum. Not in Sydney—it's still out sailing the harbor every weekend. You can join in the hauling, heaving, and coiling of the ropes, or simply roam around the deck and admire the view. *See p 24.*

**❼ Watching the flying foxes swarm above the Sydney Harbour Bridge at sunset.** Okay, it's a bit

*Sunset at Watson's Bay.*

batty (pun intended), but it's a ritual unique to Sydney. Every night thousands of gray-headed flying foxes (fruit bats) leave their daytime roosts in the Botanic Gardens and head out to hunt. Combine it with a sunset cocktail at the Opera Bar beneath the Opera House before taking in a show and you've got a quintessential Sydney moment. *See p 11.*

**8 Scaring yourself silly on a nighttime ghost tour of The Rocks.** Even if you don't believe in the life hereafter, this walking tour of Sydney's oldest neighborhood makes history come alive in a way no museum ever will. Better yet, it gives you access to some of the city's best archaeological sites normally kept under lock and key—and it includes a free beer afterward. *See p 55.*

**9 Facing your fears and diving with the sharks during feeding time at Oceanworld Manly.** This gives the term shark bait a whole new meaning, but it's the best place to get nose-to-nose with Jaws and live to tell the tale. Best not to watch the movie before you go. *See p 20.*

**10 Finding a designer bargain at Saturday's Paddington Markets.** A whole swag of Australia's top names in fashion sold their first designer duds at these churchyard markets, and it's still the best place to find a hot new label before it becomes famous—or expensive. It gets crowded, so go early and follow it up with more retail therapy along Oxford Street. *See p 76.*

**11 Doing laps in one of Sydney's harbor- or beachside swimming**

*Thrills and chills on a Rocks ghost tour.*

*Swimming with sharks, Oceanworld Manly.*

**pools.** They're cold, old, and crumbling, there are no fancy changing rooms, and there are often small sea creatures lurking in the depths, but these outdoor pools are cheap as chips and all have five-star views. *See p 87.*

⓬ **Eating fine fish and chips on the beach at Watsons Bay.** The famous beachfront Doyles seafood

*Barista at a coffee shop in Newtown.*

restaurant is a bit overhyped, but the takeaway kiosk on the wharf sells pretty much the same food for half the price, making it some of the best-value fish and chips in Sydney. *See p 32.*

⓭ **Catching a classic movie under the summer stars.** Bring your own blanket, chair, beer, wine, and nibbles to one of several parks that become outdoor movie theaters during the summer months. Don't forget the insect repellent. *See p 120.*

⓮ **Blowing the budget on dinner with a view.** It's not a cheap night out, but you'll never forget a meal at one of Sydney's fine-dining restaurants on the harbor's edge at Circular Quay. *See p 96.*

⓯ **Watching the passing street parade from a coffee shop in Newtown.** You'll never know who or what you'll see in this colorful unconventional inner-city suburb. It's people-watching at its best and costs next to nothing. *See p 63.* ●

# 1

# The Best **Full-Day Tours**

# The Best **in One Day**

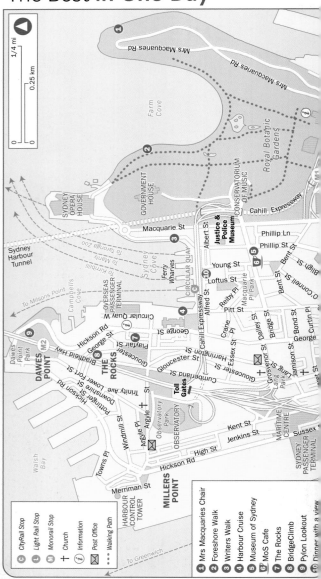

1/4 mi
0.25 km

Mrs Macquaries Rd
Mrs Macquaries Rd

Farm Cove

Royal Botanic Gardens

GOVERNMENT HOUSE

CONSERVATORIUM OF MUSIC

SYDNEY OPERA HOUSE

Macquarie St

Cahill Expressway

Justice & Police Museum

Albert St

Phillip Ln

Phillip St

Young St

Sydney Harbour Tunnel

To Kirribilli
To Manly
To Taronga Zoo

Sydney Cove

Ferry Wharves

CIRCULAR QUAY

Loftus St

Reiby Pl

Macquarie Pl Park

Bent St

Bligh St

O'Connell St

To Milsons Point

Campbells Cove

OVERSEAS PASSENGER TERMINAL

Alfred St

Pitt St

Crane Pl

Dalley St

Bridge St

Bond St

Curtin Pl

To Mosman

Circular Quay W

George St

Cahill Expressway

Essex St

Grosvenor St

Jamison St

George

Dawes Point Park

Hickson Rd

George St

THE ROCKS

Gloucester St

Gloucester St

Harrington St

Cumberland St

Laing

Lang Park

DAWES POINT

M2

Bradfield Hwy

Trinity Ave

Lower Fort St

Playfair St

Toll Gates

Hickson Rd

Pottinger St

Downshire St

Windmill St

Argyle St

Argyle Pl

Observatory Park

OBSERVATORY

Kent St

Jenkins St

MARITIME CENTRE

SYDNEY PASSENGER TERMINAL

Sussex

Walsh Bay

Towns Pl

High St

Hickson Rd

MILLERS POINT

Merriman St

HARBOUR CONTROL TOWER

To Greenwich

**Legend**

- C CityRail Stop
- L Light Rail Stop
- M Monorail Stop
- + Church
- i Information
- ⊠ Post Office
- ··· Walking Path

1 Mrs Macquaries Chair
2 Foreshore Walk
3 Writers Walk
4 Harbour Cruise
5 Museum of Sydney
6 MoS Cafe
7 The Rocks
8 BridgeClimb
9 Pylon Lookout
10 Dinner with a view

*Previous page: Sydney Harbour, also known as Port Jackson.*

On this 1-day very-best-of-Sydney tour, we don't stray very far from the harbor's edge, but you'll still need to get an early start to fit it all in. We take in all the very best views, from a convict-carved chair in a cliff to a harbor cruise, and top-of-the-city vistas from the crown of the famous Sydney Harbour Bridge. In between, discover the city's convict beginnings and finish off with a special night out at a harborside restaurant. START: **Train to Martin Place and walk to the Royal Botanic Gardens.**

**1** ★★★ **Mrs. Macquaries Chair.** Wrapped around Farm Cove, the Royal Botanic Gardens and surrounding Domain have been parklands ever since Sydney was first settled. It was set aside by Governor Phillip as his private reserve in 1788, just weeks after the First Fleeters set up camp in Sydney Cove. In 1810, Governor Macquarie ordered convicts to carve a ledge in the sandstone on the eastern point of the cove so his wife could admire the view, which today looks across to the Sydney Opera House, Harbour Bridge, and Fort Denison. ⏱ *45 min. Go early to avoid the stream of brides who flock here to have their photos taken. Also gorgeous at night. Mrs. Macquaries Rd., Mrs. Macquaries Point. Train: Circular Quay. Free admission.*

**2** ★★★ **Foreshore Walk.** From Mrs. Macquaries Chair, follow the path along the curve of Farm Cove and around the base of the Opera House to Circular Quay. ⏱ *20 min. Avoid lunchtime when jogging office workers hit the track. Free admission.*

**3** ★★ **Writers Walk.** Once past the Opera House, keep an eye out for the bronze plaques embedded in the footpath on both the eastern and western arms of Circular Quay. Each of the 50 discs has a quote about Sydney by famous writers. ⏱ *10 min. Circular Quay. Free admission.*

**4** ★★ **Harbor Cruise.** No trip to Sydney is complete without a harbor cruise, and there are several cruise operators that run cruises of varying lengths and itineraries, many of which include morning or afternoon tea, lunch, or dinner—and all provide commentary. For those on a budget, try a trip on one of the many ferries and river cats that crisscross the harbor to

*The view from Mrs. Macquaries Chair.*

*Dorothea Mackellar Plaque on the Writers Walk.*

Balmain, the North Shore, Manly, and Parramatta. ⏱ 1½–3 hr. **Train: Circular Quay. Admission $30–$185. Bookings not necessary.**

**⑤ ★★ Museum of Sydney.** Built on the ruins of Australia's first governor-general's house, the Museum of Sydney explores colonial and contemporary Sydney through found objects, video, and changing exhibitions. Even if you don't go inside, take a wander around the *Edge of the Trees* sculpture in the forecourt to hear Koori (Aboriginal) voices reciting the names of places that have today been swallowed up by the modern

*Aboriginal Culture Cruise.*

city. ⏱ *1 hr. Corner Phillip & Bridge sts. ☎ 02/9251 5988. www.hht.net. au/museums. Admission $10 adults, $5 kids. Open daily 9:30am–5pm. Train: Circular Quay.*

Take a seat outside at **⑥ MoS Cafe** and soak up the sun with a coffee, glass of wine, or a light meal if you're hungry. There's plenty of room for the kids to burn off steam while you watch in the museum forecourt. *Corner Bridge & Phillip sts. ☎ 02/9241 3636. $$–$$$.*

**⑦ ★★ The Rocks.** Sydney's oldest suburb and historic heart was once a slum full of shanghaied sailors, criminals, prostitutes, and all sorts of undesirables, including the plague in 1901. Many of the old sandstone buildings and historic pubs remain, including Sydney's oldest surviving building, and—if you believe the legends—lots of ghosts. You can easily spend a full day exploring the many museums and galleries here, but at the very least take a walk down George Street and underneath Harbour Bridge to Observatory Hill for great

views across the western reaches of the harbor. For more on The Rocks, see p 52. 🕐 *2 hr. Train: Circular Quay.*

**⑧ ★★★ Sydney Harbour Bridge Climb at Sunset.** It's a long way down from the top of Sydney Harbour Bridge (134m/440 ft.), but the view is unbeatable, especially as the sun sets and the city's lights turn on. The climb begins with a briefing in BridgeClimb's training center, where you are provided with a climbing suit, gloves, and a beanie if the weather is cold, and a harness that is later affixed to a stationary line on the catwalk. You'll also be breath-tested, so avoid alcohol before the climb. Once ready, it's out on the catwalk to the pylon and climbing up the ladder (the hardest and scariest bit) and on to the arch itself, where any fear or anxiety disappears as you take in the views. The Discovery Climb takes you through, rather than over, the steel arches and is a good alternative. Both are easy walks, just lots of steps, and the going is slow so there are plenty of stops along the way to catch your breath and take in the awesome views. At all times you are attached to the stationary line, and there is a handrail for extra support. You will need to wear rubber-soled shoes and book at least 2 weeks in advance (you can book online). It's expensive, but it's one of those once-in-a-lifetime experiences you'll never forget. 🕐 *2¼–3½ hr. Dawn, daylight, express, twilight, and night climbs available. 3 Cumberland St.* ☎ *02/8274 7777. www.bridgeclimb. com. Admission $198–$298 adults, $138–$198 kids (11 and over). Open daily except New Year's Eve. Train: Circular Quay.*

**⑨ ★ Pylon Lookout.** If Bridge-Climb is beyond your budget, you can walk across the bridge to Milsons Point train station for free then

*Market at The Rocks.*

catch the train back to the city. Stop en route to climb the 200 steps to the top of the southeast Pylon Lookout, for views almost (but not quite) as good as those from the top of the arch. The pylon lookout also features exhibitions on the history and construction of the bridge, which is the largest single arch bridge in the world and was officially opened in 1932 (although the ribbon was cut by a dashing mounted guardsman who appeared out of nowhere brandishing a sword, much to the consternation of the premier and other officials). 🕐 *45–90 min. Access to pedestrian walkway via Cumberland St. Pylon lookout admission: $11 adults & kids 14 and over, kids $4, kids 3 and under free. Open daily 10am–5pm. Train: Circular Quay.*

**⑩ ★★★ Dinner with a View.** Splash out and treat yourself to dinner at a harborside restaurant and soak in those spectacular views, but make sure you avoid the restaurants opposite the ferry wharves at Circular Quay. Best bets include ARIA ($$$$$; p 96), Quay ($$$$$; p 102), Cafe Sydney ($$$$; p 98), or if on a budget, head across the bridge to Ripples at Milsons Point, where the view is just as good and meals are all under $33 (p 102).

# The Best **in Two Days**

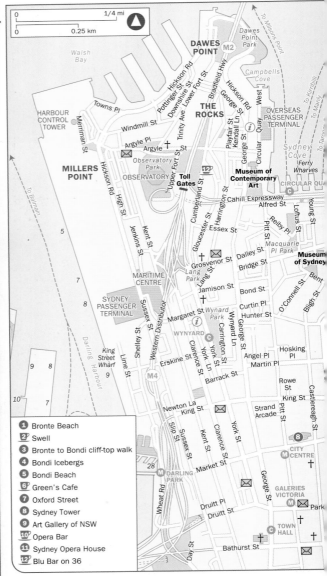

- **1** Bronte Beach
- **2** Swell
- **3** Bronte to Bondi cliff-top walk
- **4** Bondi Icebergs
- **5** Bondi Beach
- **6** Green's Cafe
- **7** Oxford Street
- **8** Sydney Tower
- **9** Art Gallery of NSW
- **10** Opera Bar
- **11** Sydney Opera House
- **12** Blu Bar on 36

**Bondi & Bronte**

Blair St
Curlewis St
O'Brien St **6**
St Francis St
Campbell Parade
**BONDI BEACH**
O'Brien St **5**
**4**
*Bondi Bay*
**3**
*Tamarama Bay*
Bronte Rd **1**
*Nelson Bay*
**2** **BRONTE**

0 ———— 1/4 mi
0 ———— 0.25 km

SYDNEY OPERA HOUSE **11** **10**

*Sydney Harbour Tunnel*

Macquarie St
Circular Quay E

*Farm Cove*

GOVERNMENT HOUSE

ert St
**Justice & Police Museum**

Phillip Ln

Cahill Expressway

CONSERVATORIUM OF MUSIC

*Royal Botanic Gardens*

Mrs Macquaries Rd

Cowper Wharf Rd
Wylde St
St Neot Ave
McDonald Ln
Challis Ave

STATE LIBRARY HOUSE OF NSW **M1**

Macquarie St

PARLIAMENT HOUSE

Hospital Rd

Art Gallery Rd

**9**

*The Domain*

Lincoln Crescent

Bland St
Nicholson St
Wilson St
Plunkett St

Dowling St
McElhone St
Brougham St
Victoria St

Hughes St

Griffiths St

Harmer St
Stephen St
Orwell St

**KINGS CROSS**

**ARTIN LACE**

**Sydney Hospital**

Queens **The Mint**
- Square **Museum**

James Rd

**ST JAMES**

St Marys Rd

Sir John Young Crescent

**WOOLLOOMOOLOO**

Cathedral St

Sylvia Chase Square

*Hyde Park*

College St

Phillip Park

Cook Park

William St

Riley St
Crown St
Palmer St
Talbot Pl
William Ln
Forbes St
Judge St

Bourke St
Forbes St
Clapton Pl

**Australian Museum**

Yurong Ln

Yurong St

Roselea Ln

*Pool of Reflection*

NZAC
MORIAL

**7**

Stanley Ln
Stanley St
Francis St
Chapel St

**C** CityRail Stop
**L** Light Rail Stop
**M** Monorail Stop
**†** Church
**✚** Hospital
**(i)** Information
**✉** Post Office
- - - Walking Path

**H**ead to Sydney's most famous beach on your second day, having seen the icons of Sydney Harbour in your day-one forays. Step out with a morning walk along the stunning Bronte to Bondi cliff-top walk, followed by a spot of retail therapy, before heading back to the city center for some art and entertainment under the soaring sails of the Opera House where you can drink in the views with a sunset cocktail at one of the city's most stylish bars.
START: Bus 378 from Railway Square to Bronte.

**① kids Breakfast on the Beach.** Start your day with a leisurely breakfast (and early morning swim if the weather is kind) on the beach at Bronte. Often overshadowed by its flashier and noisier big brother Bondi, Bronte has a more relaxed feel to it and there is a beautiful park with a great children's playground flanking the beach. ⏱ 1 hr. Weekends can get very busy as this is a popular brunching place for locals. Bus: 378.

**② ★★ Swell** is a great little cafe right on the beach where the toasted banana bread with ricotta and fresh berries takes the hard work out of making sure you get a healthy start to the day. See p 103.

**③ ★★★ Bronte to Bondi Cliff-Top Walk.** This spectacular 3.5km (2-mile) walkway linking two of the city's most famous beaches is a must-do. It's an easy to medium walk, mostly along the cliff edge. The walkway begins on the northern headland of Bronte Beach, traverses the tiny but perfectly formed Tamarama Beach (known as "Glamarama" to the locals—this is where the bold and the beautiful strut their stuff), and skirts the headland of Mackenzies Bay to the southern end of Bondi Beach. It's one sweeping view after another. Look out for

Aboriginal rock carvings of sharks and whales in the rocks beside the path. You may well see real whales in the winter months, and for 3 weeks in late October and early November the route is lined with more than 100 sculptures as part of the annual Sculpture by the Sea exhibition (p 163). The pathway is not fenced, so keep an eye on your kids. ⏱ 90 min. Avoid the early morning and late afternoon rush hours when the locals hit the track for their daily constitutional—negotiating the crush of power walkers, joggers, and dog walkers can be intense. Bus: 378.

**④ ★★ Bondi Icebergs.** This iconic ocean pool at the southern end of the beach is home to the Bondi Icebergs, founded in 1929, originally as a way for local surf lifesavers to keep fit during the winter months. To be a member you have to compete in the open-air ocean pool on 3 winter Sundays out of 4, for a period of 5 years—and if the water's not deemed cold enough ice blocks will be added. You can watch the action on Sunday mornings (first weekend in May to the last weekend in Sept) from 10:15am (spectator fee $3). The pool is open to the public (winter and summer) and the clubhouse is now home to one of the hippest bars and restaurants in the city, Icebergs Dining Room and Bar (p 100). The pool is

*Bondi Beach.*

sand is one of the best known beaches in the world, and certainly one of Australia's most famous. Cool off with a swim, or at least dip your toes in if the water's a bit chilly. If you do go in the water, stay between the red-and-yellow lifesaving flags, as the water can be treacherous if you're not used to swimming in the surf. ⏱ *1 hr. Bus: 380.*

Bondi's main drag is lined with cafes and takeaway joints, but sadly, many are best avoided unless you like to pay a lot of money for crappy coffee and off-hand service. Stay well clear of those in the center section of the strip and head instead for the far northern and southern ends or a few blocks west. ⑥ **Green's Cafe** is popular with locals in the know and a good place for coffee or a light snack. *140 Glenayr Ave.* ☎ *02/9130 6181. $.*

closed for cleaning every Thursday. *1 Notts Ave.* ☎ *02/9130 4804. Admission $5.50 adults, $3.50 kids. Mon–Fri 6am–6:30pm; Sat–Sun 6:30am–6:30pm.*

⑤ ★★ **Bondi Beach.** The 1km-long (⅔-mile) crescent of golden

⑦ **Oxford Street.** Catch the bus from Bondi Beach to Oxford Street, getting off at Paddington (Queen

*Touring Sydney Tower.*

*Shopping at Alistair Trung, in Paddington*

St.). Known as Sydney's "Style Mile" this is where many of Sydney's top designers first cut their fashion teeth. It's crammed with hip fashion boutiques and homewares shops as well as top-name designers. The side streets are lined with beautiful old terrace houses, many housing great boutiques (William St. in particular), and historic old

pubs are tucked around leafy corners. The Darlinghurst (or western end of Oxford St.) is grungier and edgier, and the upmarket designer boutiques are replaced with street fashion, books, art supplies, and music, but it's nowhere near as attractive as the Paddington end—so jump on a bus into the city once you get to South Dowling/Victoria streets. 🕐 *2 hr. Bus: 378 or 380.*

**❽ kids ★ Sydney Tower.** Take the lift up to the Observation Deck of Sydney Tower—250m (820 ft.) above the city streets—for 360-degree views of the city, harbor, and surrounding suburbs. The view is the draw card, but the ticket also includes OzTrek, a virtual reality ride featuring iconic Australian landscapes. 🕐 *50 min. Corner Pitt & Market sts.* ☎ *02/9333 9222. www.sydneytower.com.au. Admission $25 adults, $15 children, 3 and under free. Combined tickets are available with Sydney Wildlife World and Sydney Aquarium (p 39, ❷ and ❸), saving 20%. Open daily 9am–10:30pm. Train: Town Hall.*

*Art Gallery of NSW.*

*Opera House, Bennelong Point.*

**9 ★★★ Art Gallery of NSW.**
This Australian art collection holds works by some of the most loved Australian painters and sculptors and is a great introduction to both colonial and modern Australian art. There is also a very good Aboriginal collection in the third-floor Yiribana gallery. ⏱ *45 min.* *See p 28,* **4**.

**10 Your Hotel Room.** You've covered a lot of ground today, so head back to your hotel room to rest your weary feet, wash off the salt if you've been swimming, and put on some glad rags for tonight's entertainment. If you're feeling energetic, skip the hotel and proceed directly to **11** below.

Set on the lower concourse of the Opera House, the **11 ★★★ Opera Bar** is the best alfresco place to watch the sun set behind Harbour Bridge. The tasting plate for two makes a great pretheater meal. *See p 113.*

**12 ★★★ A Show at the Sydney Opera House.** Despite the name, it's not all high-brow opera that is performed in this architectural masterpiece; you can catch anything from contemporary Australian drama to a rock concert here. ⏱ *2–4 hr. See p 127.*

Nightcap with a view at **13 ★★★ Blu Bar on 36.** *See p 111.*

# The Best **in Three Days**

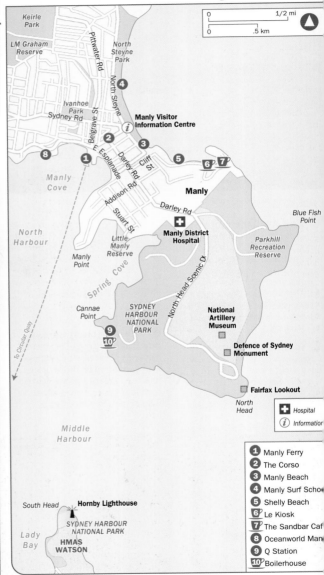

**Hospital** ➕

**Information** (i)

1 Manly Ferry
2 The Corso
3 Manly Beach
4 Manly Surf Schoo
5 Shelly Beach
6 Le Kiosk
7 The Sandbar Caf
8 Oceanworld Man
9 Q Station
10 Boilerhouse

The ferry to Manly is one of the best-value harbor cruises in the world, and the start of your third day in Sydney. Spend the morning learning how to surf on one of the city's favorite beaches, meet the sharks at the aquarium, and commune with ghosts at the old Quarantine Station. START: **Train to Circular Quay.**

**1** ★★★ kids **Manly Ferry.** The half-hour trip to the seaside suburb of Manly is one of the world's greatest ferry rides. It's worth doing even if you don't disembark and just make it a return trip. If it's a nice day, grab a seat outside for fantastic views of the Harbour Bridge and Opera House and be prepared for some rocking, rolling, and lurching as you cruise through the heads, especially on a stormy day. ⏱ *30 min. Avoid the morning and afternoon peak hours when the ferries are crowded with commuters. Wharf 3, Circular Quay. Ferry tickets $6.60 adults, $3.30 kids. Ferries depart approximately every 30 min. between 5:30am & midnight Mon–Fri, 6:20am Sat–Sun. Train: Circular Quay.*

**2** **The Corso.** It's in need of a makeover, but Manly's Corso, designed in 1855 and modeled after the Via del Corso in Rome, was once one of Sydney's grand promenades. *Warning:* Most of the cafes along it are overpriced and mediocre at best. ⏱ *20 min.*

**3** ★★★ **Manly Beach.** Rivaling Bondi as the city's most popular beach, the .6km (1-mile) stretch of sand never feels too crowded, although the safe swimming section between the flags can be elbow-to-elbow on summer weekends. On weekdays, you'll have the water almost to yourself. *North Steyne.*

**4** ★★★ kids **Manly Surf School.** If you've never surfed before, Manly is a great place to learn. The Manly Surf School runs lessons every day in winter and summer for both adults and kids and will have you standing up on your board in no time. They provide the boards and wetsuits. ⏱ *2 hr. North Steyne Surf Lifesaving Club, opposite Pine St. on the right of the surf club.* ☎ *02/9977 6977. www. manlysurfschool.com. Admission $60 adults, $50 kids. 4 lessons daily, times vary, bookings essential.*

**5** ★★★ kids **Shelly Beach.** From the southern end of Manly Beach, walk down Marine Parade to tiny Shelly Beach, a sheltered north-facing pocket of sand. It's overlooked by most visitors, but a favorite among locals, especially

*Ferries in Sydney Harbour.*

*Manly Surf School.*

those with kids. It's also a terrific snorkeling spot with lots of fish, and there are free gas barbecues and picnic facilities. Keep an eye out for the marine-inspired sculptures along Cabbage Tree Bay. 🕘 *10 min.*

Perfect for lunch (and kids), **6** ★★★ **Le Kiosk** is right on the beach in an historic sandstone cottage. It has killer views—and food to match. But if you feel a bit too sandy and salty for a sit-down affair, **7** ★★ **the Sandbar Cafe** is an inexpensive takeaway outlet run by Le Kiosk. It's a great casual alternative for a burger and beer or fish and chips on the deck. Le Kiosk is closed Tuesday. Cafe closes in wet weather. *1 Marine Parade.* ☎ *02/9977 4122. $$$$.*

**8** ★★ kids **Oceanworld Manly.** Find Nemo and all sorts of other marine creatures at this great little aquarium. Highlights include the shark tunnel, a colorful Great Barrier Reef display and the "Wall that Crawls," filled with all kinds of creepy crawlies. If you're really brave you can dive with the sharks (p 47). 🕘 *1–2 hr. West Esplanade, at the western end of Manly Cove.*

☎ *02/8251 7877. www.oceanworld. com.au. Admission $20 adults, $10 kids, $48 family. Daily 10am–5:30pm.*

**9** **Q Station.** Take a nighttime family ghost tour of the former quarantine station on North Head. Built in 1832, it was the entry point for arriving immigrants until 1984. Sadly, for the sick and those dying of diseases such as smallpox and TB, it was their last stop, which means there are plenty of ghosts. For less jumpy adults (aged 16 and up) the Spirit Investigator tour tries to put you in contact with the spirit world via a medium. Bundle up in winter and wear your walking shoes. 🕘 *2½ hr. North Head Scenic Dr.* ☎ *02/9466 1500. www.qstation.com.au. Spirit Investigator tour times & days vary, $49–$54. Bus: 135 from Manly Wharf. If returning to the city after the tour, order a taxi at reception to take you back to the Manly Wharf.*

The old boiler house at the Quarantine Station has been transformed into **10** **Boilerhouse,** a slick restaurant with lots of industrial design touches. Go for coffee, lunch, or dinner or combine it with one of the station's tour. *Q Station, North Head Scenic Drive.* ☎ *02/9466 1500. $$$–$$$$.* ●

# On the Water

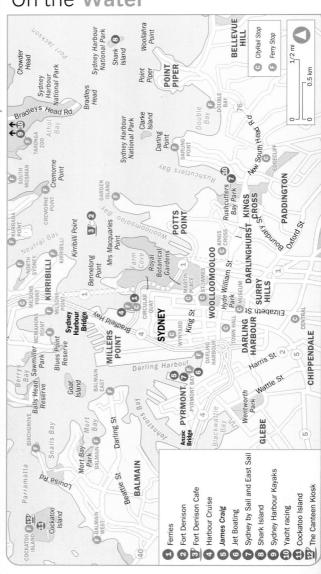

1 Ferries
2 Fort Denison
3 Fort Denison Cafe
4 Harbour Cruise
5 *James Craig*
6 Jet Boating
7 Sydney by Sail and East Sail
8 Shark Island
9 Sydney Harbour Kayaks
10 Yacht racing
11 Cockatoo Island
12 The Canteen Kiosk

*Previous page: Il Porcellino, "the little pig," at Sydney Hospital.*

Whatever the season, a day on the harbor will make you feel glad to be alive. Sydney Harbour may well be a millionaire's playground, but the good news is you don't have to be rich to see the best of it. With so many different ways to get out and about on the water you won't be able to squeeze them all into 1 day, so pick and choose from these fantastic ways to explore the best of Port Jackson and its islands. START: **Train to Circular Quay.**

**1** ★★★ kids **Ferries & River-Cats.** The average price of a ferry ticket is around $5, which makes a ride across Sydney Harbour one of the world's great bargains. A favorite trip is the half-hour run through the Heads on the Manly Ferry (p 19, **1**), but other great trips include Watsons Bay in the eastern suburbs (p 33), Mosman Bay on the lower north shore, and Balmain in the inner west. For a longer cruise, climb aboard the RiverCat for a 1-hour trip up the Parramatta River to Sydney's second-oldest settlement. ⏱ *30 min.–2 hr. return.* ☎ *131 500. www.sydney ferries.info. Admission $5.30–$6.60 adults, $2.60–$3.30 kids. Daily 6am–midnight. Train: Circular Quay.*

**2** ★ **Fort Denison.** This tiny island near the Opera House was originally a convict prison known as "Pinchgut" due to the tiny rations served there. In 1796 the executed murderer Francis Morgan was hung on a gibbet on the island's highest point as a disincentive for misbehaving. In 1857 the island was renamed Fort Denison and its round Martello Tower was one of the last to be built in the world, erected to defend Sydney against a possible attack by Russian warships, which never eventuated. The 1pm gun has been announcing lunchtime since 1906. You can visit the island on your own, but a half-hour guided tour will bring the history alive. ⏱ *1hr. Sydney Harbour, just north of the Royal Botanic Gardens.* ☎ *02/9247 5033. www. matilda.com.au. Tours $27 adults, $17 kids (including return ferry). Daily 12:15pm & 2:30pm, plus Wed–Sun 10:45am. Ferry: Circular Quay Wharf 6 & Pier 26 Darling Harbour.*

*Fort Denison, formerly Pinchgut prison.*

Okay, it might not be the best food in town (although the zucchini and corn fritters with smoked salmon are pretty good), but **3 Fort Denison Cafe** certainly has the best view. *Fort Denison, Sydney Harbour.* ☎ *02/9358 1999. $$$.*

**4 ★★ Harbor Cruise.** The same amazing scenery that you get on a ferry ride, but with commentary, and usually a cup of coffee or a meal thrown in. *See p 9,* **4**.

**5 ★★★ James Craig.** Cruise the harbor on an authentic, tall-masted sailing ship. The 19th-century, three-masted iron barque *James Craig* is one of only four of its kind anywhere in the world still sailing and one of the few that are available for day trips for landlubbers. Get involved or mooch around the deck and marvel at the hearty souls who climb aloft to the top of the masts to haul in the sails. Not suitable for under 12s. ⏲ *7 hr. Wharf 7, Pirrama Rd., Pyrmont.* ☎ *02/9298 3888. www. shf.org.au. Admission $150. Most weekends on either Sat or Sun 9:30am. Monorail: Harbourside.*

*Jet boating the harbor.*

**6 ★ Jet Boating.** Not so much a sightseeing tour, but a thrill-seeking ride. This will impress even the hardest-to-please teenager. *See p 47,* **1**.

**7 ★★★ Sail Sydney.** Sydney Harbour is a sailor's paradise and there is no better place to learn the ropes on a sunny day. Plenty of sailing outfits offer sightseeing sails on the harbor, but two of the best are Sydney by Sail and East Sail. Sit back and watch the city slip by, or trim the sails and have a try at the helm. *Sydney by Sail:* ⏲ *3hr. Festival Pontoon, next to the National Maritime Museum, Darling Harbour.* ☎ *02/ 9280 1110. www.sydneybysail.com. au. Admission $150. Daily 1pm. Monorail: Harbourside. East Sail:* ⏲ *2½ hr. d'Albora Marinas, New Beach Rd., Rushcutters Bay.* ☎ *02/9327 1166. www.eastsail. com.au. Admission $119. Daily 10am. Bus: 327.*

**8 ★ kids Shark Island.** Unpack a picnic in the middle of the harbor and pretend you're Robinson Crusoe. There are no shops on the inhabited island so make sure you take everything you need with you.

*Former shipyard on Cockatoo Island.*

🕐 *2 hr.* ☎ *02/9264 7377. www.matilda.com.au. Return ferry tickets $20 adults, $17 kids. Ferry: Circular Quay Wharf 6 & Pier 26 Darling Harbour.*

**⑨ ★★★ Sydney Harbour Kayaks.** Explore Sydney Harbour at sea level—just you, a kayak, and your paddle. Sydney Harbour Kayaks' half-day guided tour of Middle Harbour is one of the best ways to get off the beaten tourist track and explore the harbor's backwaters. It's suitable for first-time paddlers (over 12). If you don't want to join a tour you can hire a kayak and head off on your own. 🕐 *4 hr. Underneath the eastern side of the Spit Bridge, Mosman.* ☎ *02/9960 4389. www.sydneyharbourkayaks.com.au. Admission $99. Sat & Sun 8:30am. Bus: 178 from Wynyard (Stand C).*

**⑩ Yacht Racing.** Sail the harbor for the price of a couple of postrace beers. If you already know how to sail, you can try your luck at either the Cruising Yacht Club of Australia at Rushcutters Bay or the Middle Harbour Yacht Club at the Spit in Mosman as they are sometimes short of crew for their twilight races (most evenings in summer) or Sunday winter race series. Register online or simply turn up on the day.

*See websites for more details. Middle Harbour Yacht Club: www.mhyc.com.au. Cruising Yacht Club of Australia: www.cyca.com.au.*

**⑪ kids Cockatoo Island.** The largest of the harbor islands, Cockatoo has seen service as an imperial prison, industrial school, reformatory, and jail before being reborn as one of Australia's biggest shipyards. Take a self-guided tour of the former shipbuilding site, hire a kayak, or pitch a tent (you can rent camping equipment on the island) for a campsite with a million-dollar, if noisy, view. The island is also home to regular exhibitions and art installations. 🕐 *2 hr.* ☎ *02/8969 2131. www.cockatooisland.gov.au. Free admission (ferry extra). Camping $35–$50 per night for 4. Bookings* ☎ *02/8898 9774. Information center open daily 10am–4pm. Ferry: Circular Quay Wharf 5.*

**⑫ The Canteen Kiosk** offers basic cafe fare, but at least they serve good coffee. Barbecue packs are available for campers and picnickers. *Cockatoo Island, Sydney Harbour, at the junction of Parramatta & Lane Cove rivers.* ☎ *02/9810 3007. $.*

# Arty Sydney

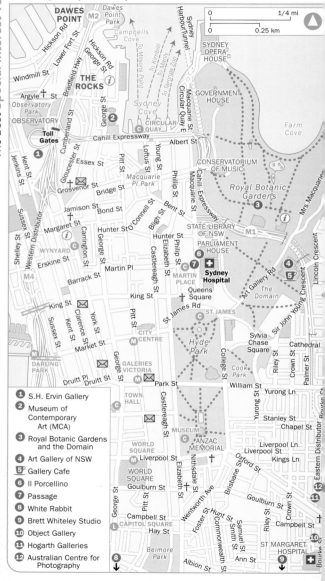

1. S.H. Ervin Gallery
2. Museum of Contemporary Art (MCA)
3. Royal Botanic Gardens and the Domain
4. Art Gallery of NSW
5. Gallery Cafe
6. Il Porcellino
7. Passage
8. White Rabbit
9. Brett Whiteley Studio
10. Object Gallery
11. Hogarth Galleries
12. Australian Centre for Photography

Sydney has a flourishing arts scene, but just like the city itself, it's far from stuffy or pretentious and most of the galleries are free. Take a crash course in the evolution of Australian art at the Art Gallery of New South Wales, check out the cutting edge at the Museum of Contemporary Art, follow an outdoor sculpture trail, and visit back-street studios in this smart arts tour of Sydney. START: **Train to Circular Quay and walk to Observatory Hill behind The Rocks.**

**❶ S.H. Ervin Gallery.** Run by the National Trust, this gallery is all about Australian art. The collection holds many pieces by iconic Australian artists and there are seven exhibitions each year. ⏱ *30 min. Watson Rd., Observatory Hill, The Rocks.* ☎ *02/ 9258 0173. www.nsw.nationaltrust. org.au. Admission $7. Tues–Sun 11am–5pm. Train: Circular Quay.*

**❷ ★ Museum of Contemporary Art (MCA).** Big, bold, bright, wonderful, and sometimes just plain weird is the best way to describe the eclectic range of works and the program of exhibitions in this museum dedicated to contemporary art. If you subscribe to the I-don't-know-much-about-art-but-I-know-what-I-like school, take one of the free guided tours and see if it makes any more sense. ⏱ *45 min. 140 George St.* ☎ *02/9245 2400. www.mca.com.au. Free admission. Daily 10am–5pm. Tours Mon–Fri*

*11am & 1pm; Sat–Sun noon & 1:30pm. Train: Circular Quay.*

**❸ ★★★ Royal Botanic Gardens and the Domain.** The Royal Botanic Gardens and the Domain have more than 35 fountains, sculptures, and memorials. Personal favorites include the soundscape installation by Nigel Helyer called *Dual Nature,* relating to the history of people and shipping in Woolloomooloo Bay. Chambers create sounds from the ocean and mix them with a solar-powered recording. Also worth finding is Janet Laurence's *Veil of Trees,* a meandering line of forest red gums with glass panels embedded with seeds, ash, honey, resin, and fragments of prose and poems by Australian writers, inspired by the landscape. You can't miss Brett Whiteley's famous matches, one live and one burnt, behind the Art Gallery of NSW. The official name is

*Exhibit at the Museum of Contemporary Art.*

*Almost Once.* ⏱ *30 min. Train: Martin Place. See p 80,* **2**.

**4** ★★★ **Art Gallery of New South Wales.** I never tire of this gallery where there's always something new. For first-time visitors it presents a snapshot of the history and evolution of Australian art, from Aboriginal and colonial through to contemporary works, as well as significant collections of European and Asian art and international blockbuster exhibitions. The best of the free guided tours is the collection highlights tour, daily at 11am (except Mon), 1pm, and 2pm. Wednesday night is Art after Hours, a changing program of free events until 9pm featuring films, talks, tours, performances, food, and wine. Chill out listening to live jazz in the ArtBar with a cocktail while you watch the sun set over Woolloomooloo. ⏱ *1hr. Art Gallery Rd., the Domain.* ☎ *02/9225 1700. www.artgallery.nsw.gov.au & www.artafterhours.com.au. Free admission. Daily 10am–5pm; Wed 9pm. Train: Martin Place (10 min. walk).*

Come to **5** **Gallery Cafe** for reasonable cafe-style food, coffee, and wine by the glass. In the Art Gallery of NSW. ☎ *02/9225 1819. $.*

**6** **Il Porcellino.** Rub the nose of the wild boar (a copy of the 500-year-old one in Florence, Italy) at the top of the hill outside Sydney Hospital for good luck. ⏱ *5 min. Macquarie St. Train: Martin Place.*

**7** **Passage.** The water sculpture by Anne Graham in Martin Place consists of three bronze balls, reflection pools and fountains, and an eerie mist that rises every 10 minutes from pavement grills. This artist's illusion of the space's past residents often disrupts traffic on Macquarie Street if the wind is blowing the wrong way. *Train: Martin Place.*

**8** ★★★ **White Rabbit.** This privately owned gallery is a four-story temple to one woman's passion for collecting contemporary Chinese art and is one of the world's largest collections. There are more than 450 artworks on show here, all post-2000; but, unlike most private galleries, they are not for sale. ⏱ *1 hr. 30 Balfour St., Chippendale.* ☎ *02/8399 2867. www.white rabbitcollection.org. Free admission. Thurs–Sun 10am–6pm. Bus: 352 or walk from Central Station.*

**9** ★★★ **Brett Whiteley Studio.** Tucked away in a back alley, the former studio of artist Brett

*Artist Anne Graham's The Passage.*

*Exhibit at the Object Gallery.*

Whiteley can be hard to find (look for the telltale matches on an otherwise plain wall), but is worth the effort. It's full of memorabilia, photographs, objects, postcards, furniture, music collections, and sketchbooks, but the main reason to visit is the changing exhibitions of the late artist's works. On Saturdays the studio is often host to a live drawing workshop, so if nudity offends, go on Sunday. 🕐 *45 min. 2 Raper St. (near Devonshire & Crown sts.), Surry Hills.* ☎ *02/9225 1881. www.brettwhiteley. org. Free admission. Sat–Sun 10am– 4pm. Bus: 301, 302, 303 from Castlereagh St. (near King St.).*

**10** ★★ **Object Gallery.** The latest in cutting-edge Australian craft and design, with everything from weird and wonderful—but definitely not wearable—clothes, to fine jewelry, furniture, and industrial design, depending on the exhibit of the day. 🕐 *30 min. 417 Bourke St., Surry Hills.* ☎ *02/9361 4511. www.object. com.au. Free admission. Tues–Fri 11am–5pm; Sat–Sun 10am–5pm.*

*Bus: 378, 380 & walk from Taylor Square.*

**11** **Hogarth Galleries.** This private gallery has been showing and selling high-end Aboriginal art since 1972, long before Aboriginal canvases became fashionable and valued. The work here's not cheap, but it's the best you'll see outside a public gallery. 🕐 *15 min. 7 Walker Lane (off Liverpool St. from Oxford St.), Paddington.* ☎ *02/9360 6839. Free admission, tour prices vary, bookings essential. Tues–Sat 10am–5pm. Bus: 378, 380.*

**12** ★★ **Australian Centre for Photography.** This is my favorite photographic gallery in Sydney. There are two gallery spaces, a foyer display area, and the Project Wall for emerging artists, many of whom are students at the center. The exhibition program is a mix of Australian and international work from both established artists and fresh talent. 🕐 *30 min. 257 Oxford St., Paddington.* ☎ *02/9332 1455. Free admission. Tues–Fri noon–7pm; Sat–Sun 10am–6pm. Bus 378, 380.*

*Australian Centre for Photography.*

# Cliff-Top Sydney

1 Coogee Beach
2 Clovelly Beach
3 Bronte to Bondi
4 Federation Cliff Walk
5 Macquarie Lighthouse
6 Doyles on the Wharf
7 Watsons Bay Hotel
8 The Gap Bluff
9 South Head
10 Lady Bay Beach
11 Camp Cove
12 Watsons Bay Ferry
13 Vaucluse House
14 Nielsen Park
15 Nielsen Park Cafe
16 Hermitage Foreshore Walk

SYDNEY HARBOUR NATIONAL PARK
Hornby Lighthouse
HMAS WATSON
Camp Cove
Laings Point
Cliff St
SYDNEY HARBOUR NATIONAL PARK
Port Jackson
Watsons Bay
The Gap
Gap Park
Vaucluse Point
Parsley Bay
Hopetoun
Dunbar Head
Vaucluse Bay
Shark Bay
Steel Point
Nielsen Park
Vaucluse Park
Old South Head Rd
Lighthouse Reserve
Christison Park
Shark Island
Hermit Bay
Vaucluse Rd
VAUCLUSE
Diamond Bay
Woollahra Point
Hermit Point
Towns Rd
POINT PIPER
Rose Bay
ROSE BAY
Lancaster Rd
Military Rd
Lyne Park
New South Head Rd
Dover Rd
Old South Head Rd
DOVER HEIGHTS
Rodney Reserve
BELLEVUE HILL
Royal Sydney Golf Course
Hardy St
Military Rd
Victoria Rd
O'Sullivan Rd
Murriverie Rd
DOUBLE BAY
Blair St
Curlewis St
BONDI BEACH
Campbell Parade
BONDI
Waverly Park
Bondi Rd
Bondi Bay
Birrell St

Area of main map

Clovelly Bay
Coogee Bay

0    1/4 mi
0    0.25 km

0    1 mi

One sweeping cliff-top view after another is the order of the day on this full-day coastal walking tour from Coogee Beach around South Head to harborside Vaucluse via Bondi and Watsons Bay. Lace up your walkers; pack your swimmers, sunscreen, and plenty of water; and step out on one of the best urban coastal walks in the world. START: **Bus 372, 373, or 374 to Coogee Beach.**

*Coogee Walk.*

**1 ★★ Coogee Beach.** Most people begin the southern cliff-top walking trail at Bronte Beach, but you can actually start two beaches to the south at Coogee and head north over Dunningham Reserve (good picnic facilities) and past Gordon's Bay, a secret little bay carved into sheer sandstone headlands, and on to Clovelly. 🕑 *30 min.*

**2 ★★★ Clovelly Beach.** More like a gigantic pool than an ocean beach, this narrow rocky channel is a great place to swim. 🕑 *30 min.*

**3 ★★★ Bronte to Bondi.** One of the best urban walks you'll find anywhere. A new cliff-hugging boardwalk just south of Bronte Beach has some superb viewing platforms and means you no longer need to walk through the cemetery. The rest of the walk is a combination of paved pathways and steps with few steep slopes or hazards (apart from dogs and joggers, and traffic on the strip linking Tamarama with Bronte). 🕑 *90 min. See p 14,* **3**.

**4 ★★★ Federation Cliff Walk.** This 5km (3-mile) walkway from Dover Heights on the northern side of Bondi to Diamond Bay (just south of Watsons Bay at the tip of South Head) is not nearly as popular or as crowded as the Bondi to Bronte section, but every bit as scenic—if not more so. There are a couple of short sections through suburban streets, but it's pretty much cliff-edge the

*Federation Cliff Walk.*

*Macquarie Lighthouse.*

entire way. There are a number of staircases to negotiate, so it's not a good walk for those with dodgy knees. ⏲ 90 min.

**5 Macquarie Lighthouse.** Australia's first lighthouse, the current incarnation (1883) is an exact copy of an earlier one designed by convict architect Francis Greenway and built on-site in 1818. ⏲ *20 min. Old South Head Rd., Vaucluse.* ☎ *02/8969 2100. 10am–4pm. Free admission. Tours $5 adults, $3 kids; every second month; bookings essential.*

*Watson's Bay beer garden.*

Treat yourself to some of the best fish and chips in town from the takeaway kiosk at **6 ★★ kids Doyles on the Wharf,** run by the legendary Doyle family, who have been dishing up fabulous seafood in Watsons Bay since 1885. Avoid weekends if you can (or at least avoid the lunchtime rush), when queues can be painfully long. *Fishermans Wharf.* ☎ *02/9337 6214. $.*

Next, rest your legs at one of Sydney's best beer gardens at **7 ★ Watsons Bay Hotel,** a popular spot on Sunday afternoons. They do great burgers. *1 Military Rd.* ☎ *02/9337 5444. $.*

**8 Gap Bluff.** One of the most popular cliff-top lookouts in Sydney, these sheer cliffs plunge more than 80m (262 ft.) into roiling waves. Unfortunately, it was the site of Sydney's worst maritime tragedy when the *Dunbar* was shipwrecked here in 1857 with the loss of 121 passengers and crew. The sole survivor was washed overboard and wedged into a crevice on the cliffs, 10m (33 ft.) above the waves. The anchor is bolted into a sandstone ledge as part of a memorial at the northern end of the park. ⏲ *30 min. Enter from Military Rd.*

**9 ★★★ South Head.** Part of Sydney Harbour National Park, the views across the harbor to North Head are nothing short of breathtaking. There is a loop walk around the headland that takes in a number of glorious vantage points, old canons, and gun emplacements of various 19th- and 20th-century vintages. The red-and-white Hornby Lighthouse is Australia's third oldest. ⏲ *45 min. Follow the path from the end of Cliff St.*

*Sunset over Watson's Bay.*

**⑩ Lady Bay Beach.** Cover your eyes as you skirt the bay above Lady Bay Beach if you don't enjoy looking at nude bodies. It's also known as Lady Jane Beach, and clothing is strictly optional. ⏲ *5 min.*

**⑪ Camp Cove.** Popular for snorkeling, this charming little beach marks the spot where Captain Arthur Phillip first came ashore in Sydney Harbour in 1788, although you won't find much more than a plaque to commemorate the occasion. ⏲ *10 min. Cove St.*

**⑫ ★★ Watsons Bay Ferry.** If you're feeling a bit footsore, jump on the ferry at Watsons Bay for a trip back to Circular Quay. ⏲ *20 min. Admission $5.30 adults, $2.60 kids. Ferries depart approximately every 30 min. Mon–Fri, or every 45 min. Sat–Sun, btw. 10am and 3:50pm (7pm Sat–Sun).*

**⑬ ★★ Vaucluse House.** Learn about the scandals that dogged William Charles Wentworth, the famous son of a convict, and his illegitimate wife. He was one of the first to cross the Blue Mountains in 1813; he established the colony's first newspaper, founded the country's first

university, and lobbied for, and achieved, representative government for NSW—but despite his amazing achievements he and his wife and 10 children were shunned by the narrow-minded colonial society of the day. The heritage gardens will impress garden lovers. ⏲ *1 hr. See p 36,* **⑦**.

**⑭ kids ★★ Nielsen Park.** This sheltered harbor beach is flanked by shady parklands and seems to be the secret playground of the lucky locals. Go and spoil their fun by rolling out a picnic blanket and staking out some territory. Don't let the fact that the beach in Nielsen Park is called Shark Beach worry you—it has shark-proof swimming areas and is great for small kids. ⏲ *30 min. Enter via Vaucluse Rd.*

Good coffee comes with a great view at **⑮ Nielsen Park Cafe.** Opt for takeaway on the sand and try to avoid the weekend brunch crowds. *Greycliffe Ave., inside Nielsen Park.* ☎ *02/9337 7333. $.*

**⑯ Hermitage Foreshore Walk.** An easy walk through native bushland to Rose Bay with great harbor views along the way. ⏲ *30 min. Begins at Hermitage Foreshore Reserve.*

*Camp Cove.*

# Historic Sydney

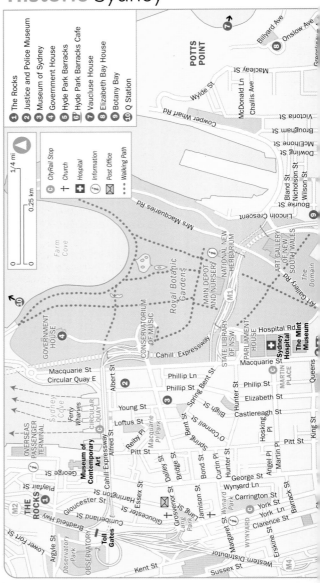

1 The Rocks
2 Justice and Police Museum
3 Museum of Sydney
4 Government House
5 Hyde Park Barracks
6 Hyde Park Barracks Cafe
7 Vaucluse House
8 Elizabeth Bay House
9 Botany Bay
10 Q Station

CityRail Stop
Church
Hospital
Information
Post Office
Walking Path

1/4 mi
0.25 km

POTTS POINT

Billyard Ave
Onslow Ave
Mackeay St
McDonald Ln
Challis Ave
Wylde St
Victoria St
Brougham St
McElhone St
Dowling St
Bland St
Nicholson St
Wilson St
Bourke St
Lincoln Crescent

Cowper Wharf Rd

Mrs Macquaries Rd

Farm Cove

Royal Botanic Gardens

MAIN DEPOT AND NURSERY

NATIONAL NEW HERBARIUM

ART GALLERY OF NEW SOUTH WALES

The Domain

Art Gallery Rd

CONSERVATORIUM OF MUSIC

GOVERNMENT HOUSE 4

Cahill Expressway

STATE LIBRARY OF NSW

PARLIAMENT HOUSE

Hospital Rd

Sydney Hospital

The Mint Museum

Macquarie St Circular Quay E

Albert St

Phillip Ln
Phillip St
Spring Bent St
Philip St

Macquarie St
MARTIN PLACE
Queens

Young St
Loftus St
Reiby Pl
Macquarie Pl Park
Hunter St
Elizabeth St
Castlereagh St
King St

Bligh St
O'Connell St
Spring St
Bent St
Hosking Pl
Pitt St

2

3

Ferry Wharves
CIRCULAR QUAY
Alfred St

Pitt St
Dalley St
Bridge St
Bond St
Curtin Pl
Hunter St
Angel Pl
Martin Pl

Sydney Cove

OVERSEAS PASSENGER TERMINAL

Museum of Contemporary Art

George St
Cahill Expressway

George St
Wynyard Ln
Carrington St
WYNYARD
York St
York Ln
Clarence St

Playfair St

THE ROCKS 1

Essex St
Harrington St
Gloucester St
Cumberland St

Grosvenor St
Jamison St
Lang Park
Margaret St
Wynyard Park

Barrack St

Argyle St
Observatory Park
OBSERVATORY

Toll Gates

Lower Fort St
Bradfield Hwy

Kent St
Sussex St
Western Distributor
Erskine St

M2

M1

M4

As the country's birthplace and first European settlement, Sydney has a rich seam of convict and colonial heritage. Hear the clanking of the convicts' chains, smell the fear of criminals past, and poke your nose into the genteel drawing rooms of the colonial elite in this collection of museums, grand harborside residences, and historic sites. START: **Train to Circular Quay and walk to The Rocks.**

**1 ★★★ The Rocks.** Much more than just an open-air museum, the past and present coexist in The Rocks, thanks mainly to a very vocal conservation campaign in the 1970s backed by unions which imposed "green bans" on redevelopment that ultimately saved the many historic buildings and homes in what was a working class area at the time. The Rocks Discovery Museum (p 53, 4) tells the story of the battle to save The Rocks and provides an overview of the area from pre-European days to now, while a guided tour of the Susannah Place Museum (p 55, 14) provides a glimpse into what it was like to live there before it became the city's most popular tourist destination. ⏲ 2 hr. Train: Circular Quay.

**2 ★★★ Justice and Police Museum.** Take a walk on the dark side at this fantastic little museum in the old police and court building (1856–88). The old cells, courtroom, prisoner docks, and spiked gates are still there, and there's usually an interesting, quirky exhibition showing, but what makes this place so wonderfully chilling is the array of confiscated weapons and forensic photographs of past crimes and bad guys, most of which was put together in 1910 as part of a collection used to instruct new constables in the wicked ways of criminals. ⏲ 1 hr. Corner Albert & Phillip sts. ☎ 02/9252 1144. www.hht.net.au. Admission $10 adults, $5 kids. Daily 9:30am–5pm. Train: Circular Quay.

**3 ★★ Museum of Sydney.** The only museum dedicated to the history of the city. See p 10, 5.

*The eerie mug shot exhibit at the Justice and Police Museum.*

*Government House.*

**❹ ★★★ Government House.**
Sydney's version of Buckingham Palace. Well, not really, but it was designed by the same architect (Edward Blore) and between 1846 and 1996 it was home to 27 successive governors, the queen's man (or these days, woman) in NSW. When the house was built it was the most sophisticated example of Gothic Revival architecture in the colony, and as you would expect, it contains a grand collection of Australian furniture and art. What you don't expect to find is the stunning collection of contemporary glass art and modern furniture mixed in with the old. ⏱ *45 min. Macquarie St. (near Bridge St., in the Royal Botanic Gardens).* ☎ *02/9931 5222. www.hht.net.au. Free admission. Guided tours every 30 min. Fri–Sun 10:30am–3pm. The house is closed when hosting a vice-regal function. Train: 10 min. walk from Circular Quay or Martin Place.*

**❺ ★★★ kids Hyde Park Barracks.** Up to 50,000 convicts have slept here (600 at any one time) but it was never a jail. The elegant 1817 sandstone building was designed by convict architect Francis Greenway, and it's the best place to go if you want to learn more about the life and harsh times of convict NSW. Cranky kids may well benefit from some time in the re-created punishment box or trying on some ankle irons for size. Many of the artifacts on display were found in rats' nests in and under the building. ⏱ *1 hr. Queens Square, Macquarie St.* ☎ *02/8239 2311. www.hht.net.au. Admission $10 adults, $5 kids. Daily 9:30am–5pm. Train: St. James or Martin Place.*

Grab a coffee beside the open fire or a cool drink in the courtyard of the **❻ Hyde Park Barracks Café.** This lovely licensed cafe in the barracks grounds also serves up a nice lunch. ☎ *02/9222 1815. $$.*

**❼ ★★ Vaucluse House.** The beautifully preserved and furnished home of one of the early colony's greatest statesmen, William Charles Wentworth. ⏱ *1 hr. Wentworth Rd., Vaucluse.* ☎ *02/9388 7922. www. hht.net.au/museums/vaucluse_ house. Admission $8 adults, $4 kids. Fri–Sun 9:30am–4pm. Bus: 325 from (and to) Circular Quay.*

**❽ ★ Elizabeth Bay House.** When it was built in the 1830s it was the grandest house in the colony despite never being finished. Fast forward 100 years and it was the scene

---

of wild and raucous booze-fueled parties when it was a bohemian artists' squat. Later it was reborn as a glamorous reception hall in 1935, converted into 16 flats during WWII, restored in the mid-1970s, and opened as a museum in 1977. Go there just to see the elegant domed saloon and geometric staircase and to admire the magnificent harbor view. ⏱ 30 min. 7 Onslow Ave., Elizabeth Bay. ☎ 02/9356 3022. www.hht.net.au. Admission $8 adults, $4 kids. Fri–Sun 9:30am–4pm. Bus: 311.

**9 Botany Bay.** Originally called Stingray Bay before being renamed Botany Bay in honor of the great quantity of plant specimens collected there, this is where then Lieutenant James Cook first stepped ashore in 1770. The landing spot is marked by a plaque and is part of the southern (Kurnell) section of Kamay Botany Bay National Park. Across the bay, the Lapérouse Museum stands on the site of the first landing of the First Fleet in January 1788, followed days later by the French explorer Comte de La Pérouse. The First Fleet had meanwhile moved on to Camp Cove and Port Jackson (p 33, **11**), having decided that Botany Bay was unfit

Elizabeth Bay House.

for settlement. ⏱ 30 min.–1 hr. at each site. Kurnell Visitor Centre: Cape Solander Dr. ☎ 02/9668 2000. Park entry $7 per vehicle if driving. Daily 9:30am–4:30pm. Bus: 987 from Cronulla train station. Lapérouse Museum: Anzac Parade, La Perouse. ☎ 02/9311 3379. Admission $5.50 adults, $3.30 kids. Thurs–Sun 10am–4pm. Bus: 394.

**10 Q Station.** Formerly Quarantine Station, the stunning historic site on North Head near Manly has a range of interactive tours that bring the history (and ghosts) alive. See p 20, **9**.

Kurnell Discovery Centre in Botany Bay.

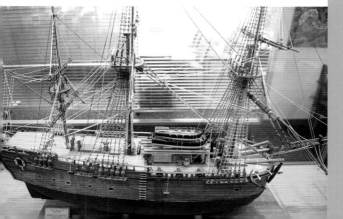

# Sydney for Kids

1. Australian Museum
2. Sydney Aquarium
3. Sydney Wildlife World
4. Tumbalong Park
5. The Powerhouse Museum
6. The Courtyard Cafe
7. Circus Arts School
8. Taronga Zoo
9. Luna Park
10. The Deck

**C** CityRail Stop
**L** Light Rail Stop
**M** Monorail Stop
† Church
✚ Hospital
ⓘ Information
✉ Post Office
- - - Walking Path

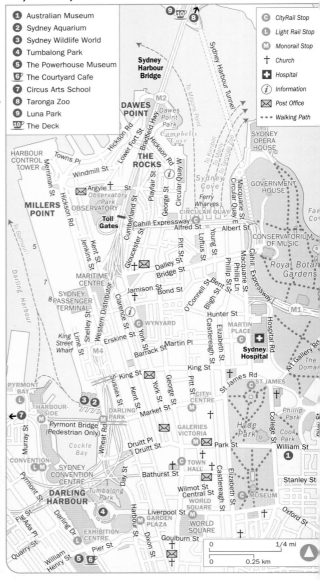

Kids love Sydney's rampaging dinosaurs, man-eating sharks, kangaroos, koalas, and creepy-crawlies. Whether you're introducing the kids to the wonders of Australia's weird wildlife, teaching them to fly on a trapeze, taking them for a roller-coaster ride, or bedding down with the animals at the zoo, there's plenty to keep kids of all ages entertained and enthralled. START: **Train to Museum Station in Hyde Park.**

**1** ★★ **Australian Museum.** Most kids head straight for the dinosaurs, museum mummy, or skeletons, depending on their age and penchant for ghoul. They also like the Notorious Australian Insects and Spiders display on level 2—Australian Upside-Down Fly or Hairy Cicada anyone? For tiny tots, the under-5's "pods" let them get their hands on things you wouldn't normally dream of letting them play with. ⏱ *2 hr. 6 College St. (opposite Hyde Park).* ☎ *02/9320 6000. www.austmus. gov.au. Admission $12 adults, $6 kids. Daily 9:30am–5pm. Train: Museum.*

**2** ★★★ **Sydney Aquarium.** Little kids come here to find Nemo (there are clownfish here in abundance so they won't be disappointed) while bigger kids usually have to be dragged away from the glass underwater tunnel inside the shark exhibit, especially if it's feeding time. Other highlights include

coral reef and tropical fish exhibits, seals, saltwater crocodiles, and penguins. For an additional $5 you can ride a glass-bottomed boat across the shark tank, but it's not nearly as exciting as the posters will have you believe. ⏱ *90 min. Aquarium Pier, Darling Harbour.* ☎ *02/8251 7800. www.sydneyaquarium.com.au. Admission $35 adults, $18 kids. Tickets 10% cheaper online. A Combo Pass gives entry into Aquarium and Sydney Wildlife World (or Sydney Tower) and saves 20% of the total cost and is valid for 30 days, so you don't have to visit them all on 1 day. Daily 9am–8pm. Train: Wynyard.*

**3** ★★ **Sydney Wildlife World.** This is the place to see koalas, kangaroos, emus, platypuses, and all of our deadly snakes and spiders. The walk-though enclosures allow you to get up close and you can even have your photo taken petting a koala (not cuddling—that's illegal in NSW) or with a (nonvenomous) snake

*The Locomotive No. 1 exhibit illustrates the age of steam travel, The Powerhouse Museum.*

385,000 objects (so they tell me . . . I haven't counted) relating to history, science, technology, design, industry, decorative arts, music, transport, and space exploration. There's always a good, and often quirky, exhibition or two and they're always hands-on and interactive, so it's a winner with easily bored kids. ⏱ *1 hr., but you could easily spend all day here. 500 Harris St.* ☎ *02/9217 0111. www.powerhousemuseum. com. Admission $10 adults, $5 kids. Daily 10am–5pm. Monorail: Paddys Market.*

In the courtyard on level 1 of the museum is the kid-friendly 6 **Courtyard Cafe.** They don't even mind too much if you feed the kids food you have brought with you, and tables are within sight of the playground, so they can play while you relax with your coffee and enjoy a snack from the cafe. *In the Power-house Museum.* ☎ *02/9217 0111. $.*

*Trapeze skills at Circus Arts School.*

draped around your neck. Just be careful not to pick up any hitchhiking butterflies on your way out. ⏱ *90 min. Next door to Sydney Aquarium at Darling Harbour.* ☎ *02/9333 9288. www.sydneywild lifeworld.com.au. Admission $35 adults, $18 kids. Tickets 10% cheaper online and combined tickets are available, see* 2, *above. Daily 9am–5pm. Monorail: Darling Park.*

4 **Tumbalong Park.** Keeping the kids amused all day can be expensive, so Tumbalong Park is a great place to give your wallet a rest and let the kids burn off some excess energy in the playground and splashing in the fountains if it's hot. Highlights include a giant climbing net, balancing beams, a spinning wheel, tunnels, and a 21m (69-ft.) "flying fox" (or zip-line swing). ⏱ *30 min. Southern section of Darling Harbour. Free admission. Monorail: Darling Park.*

5 ★★★ **Powerhouse Museum.** There's something for everyone in this huge museum, with more than

*Giraffes with a view at Taronga Zoo.*

**7 Circus Arts School.** Teach the kids to fly on the trapeze. Classes are suitable for anyone over the age of 6, and no previous flying experience is necessary. **Warning:** When you see how much fun they're having you'll want to have a go, too. ⏱ *90 min. Olympic Blvd., Sydney Olympic Park.* ☎ *0412 402 742. www.circusarts.com.au. Lessons $55. See website for class times. Train: Sydney Olympic Park.*

**8 ★★ Taronga Zoo.** One of the most beautifully sited zoos in the world with million-dollar harbor views. If you just want to see Australian wildlife then the new Sydney Wildlife World (see **3**, above) is probably a better bet, but if the kids are keen to see elephants, gorillas, bears, lions, and more, come here. Half the fun is the trip on the ferry and Sky Safari Cable Car from the wharf. The overnight **★★★ Roar & Snore** program is excellent. It includes guided tours, dinner, and accommodations in a tent (provided), and you can hire sleeping bags—but kids must be at least 5 years old. ⏱ *3 hr. Bradleys Head Rd., Mosman.* ☎ *02/9969 2777. www.zoo.nsw.gov.au. Admission $44 adults, $22 kids. Zoo Pass combines ferry, cable car, and zoo entry for $50 adults, $25 kids, $140 family. Daily 9am–5pm. Roar & Snore:* ☎ *02/9978 4791. $175 adults, $110 kids. Bookings essential. Ferry: From Circular Quay.*

**9 ★★ Luna Park.** The big smiling face at the gate of Luna Park has been a Sydney icon (in various incarnations) since 1935. Little kids like the carousel and Coney Island,

*Iconic Luna Park.*

bigger kids prefer the high-octane rides like the Wild Mouse roller coaster and the Flying Saucer. I like hanging upside down in midair as the Rotor's floor drops away. ⏱ *1 hr. 1 Olympic Dr., Milsons Point.* ☎ *02/ 9033 7676. www.lunaparksydney. com. Free admission, some rides extra. Mon 11am–4pm; Fri 11am– 11pm; Sat 10am–11pm; Sun 10am– 6pm. Closed Tues–Thurs; open daily during school holidays. Train: Milsons Point or ferry from Circular Quay.*

If your kids are old enough to roam the rides on their own, sneak into the grown-up bar called **10 ★ the Deck** and enjoy a well-earned glass of wine with a fantastic city and harbor view. Just inside the face at Luna Park. ☎ *02/9033 7670. $$.*

# Aboriginal Sydney

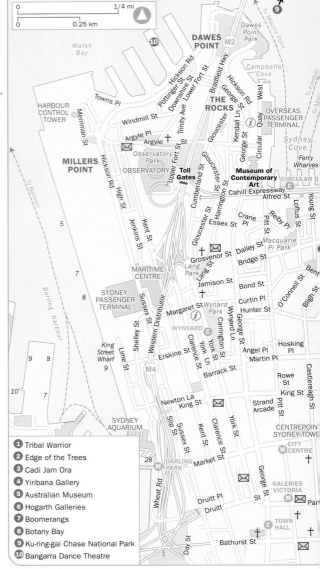

1 Tribal Warrior
2 Edge of the Trees
3 Cadi Jam Ora
4 Yiribana Gallery
5 Australian Museum
6 Hogarth Galleries
7 Boomerangs
8 Botany Bay
9 Ku-ring-gai Chase National Park
10 Bangarra Dance Theatre

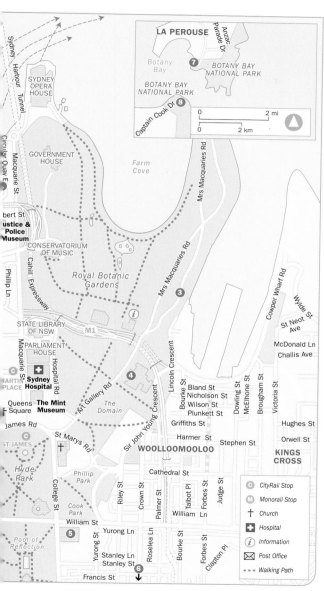

Sydney will never the look the same once you've seen it though Aboriginal eyes! The Eora lived, hunted, and celebrated in the place we now call Sydney for more than 40,000 years before the white man came. You have to dig a little, but there's more to Aboriginal Sydney than mass-produced tourist tat. It's a different world view, and one that many (white) locals don't even know exists.
START: **Train to Circular Quay.**

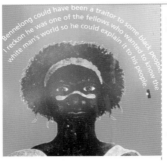

*Bennelong could have been a traitor to some black people. I reckon he was one of the fellows who wanted to know the white man's world so he could explain it to his people*

*The story line at Cadi Jam Ora, (First Encounters Garden).*

**1 ★ kids Tribal Warrior.** The Eora call Sydney Harbour Birra Birra, just one of the things you'll learn on this cultural harbor cruise, along with an eye-opening alternative history of Sydney. A highlight is the visit to Clark Island. It's not super-slick, seldom runs on time, and many of the stories are personal stories about growing up in communities a long way from Sydney, but it's a great way to meet and chat one-on-one with Aboriginal people and learn about their belief systems. 🕐 2 hr. Circular Quay Wharf 6. ☎ 02/9206 1111. www.captaincook. com.au/TRIBAL. Admission $60 adults, $45 kids. Wed–Sun 3pm (1pm Apr–Oct). Train: Circular Quay.

**2 Edge of the Trees.** See p 10, **5**.

**3 Cadi Jam Ora.** Also called the First Encounters gardens, these gardens showcase the many Aboriginal uses of native plants. The grounds were once an important ceremonial site and the scene of many of the first (and often tragic) encounters between Europeans and the local Cadigal people. A 52m (171-ft.) "storyline" tells the Aboriginal history of Sydney from the Dreaming to the present, compiled from more than 40 interviews with local Aboriginal people. Take a self-guided tour or take a tour with an Aboriginal guide. 🕐 1 hr. Royal Botanic Gardens, Mrs. Macquaries Rd. ☎ 02/9231 8134. Prices vary, bookings essential. Train: Martin Place or Circular Quay.

**4 ★★★ Yiribana Gallery.** Permanent display of Aboriginal and Torres Strait Islander art at the Art Gallery of NSW. See p 28, **4**.

**5 Australian Museum.** Indigenous Australians is the name of an exhibition examining both the traditional and spiritual aspects of Aboriginal culture as well as many

*Aboriginal art, Australian Museum.*

*James Cook bust, Kurnell Discovery Centre.*

of the problems and issues they have faced since colonization, including the Stolen Generation, when Government policy dictated the forcible removal of children from their families until as recently as the 1970s. Prime Minister Rudd finally apologized for this atrocity in early 2008. ⏱ *1 hr. See p 39,* ❶.

❻ **Hogarth Galleries.** *See p 29,* ⓫.

❼ **Botany Bay.** Site of the first contact between the crew of James Cook's *Endeavour* and the Aboriginal people of Australia in 1770. The Kurnell Discovery Centre has a permanent exhibit about the contact called "Eight Days that Changed the World." *See p 37,* ❾.

❽ **Aboriginal Heritage Museum.** There are thousands of Aboriginal sites scattered around Sydney, but unless you know what you're looking for, they are all too easy to walk past. The staff at this little museum will show you how you can find them and what to look for. It also has a vast collection of

Aboriginal artifacts on display. ⏱ *30 min. 39/137-145 Sailors Bay Rd., Northbridge.* ☎ *02/9949 9882. www.aboriginalheritage.org. Free admission. Mon–Fri 9am–4pm. Bus: 202, 203, 205, 206, 207, 208 from the Wynyard.*

❾ **Ku-ring-gai Chase National Park.** There are more than 800 Aboriginal sites in this park in the northern suburbs of Sydney. They include rock engravings, burial sites, ax grinding grooves, and places that show evidence of Aboriginal occupation. ⏱ *2–4 hr. See p 81,* ❽. *Train: Berowra. Bus: 190 from Wynyard to Palm Beach. Ferry: Palm Beach Wharf to the Basin.*

❿ ★★★ **Bangarra Dance Theatre.** Go out of your way to catch a performance of this amazing Indigenous dance troupe if they are in town. Melding 40,000 years of dance traditions and storytelling with stunning contemporary dance, their performance will leave you breathless, inspired, challenged, and a whole array of other emotions. They tour extensively, and tickets sell out fast. ⏱ *2–3 hr. The Wharf, Walsh Bay, Sydney Harbour. www. bangarra.com.au. Ticket prices vary.*

*Bangarra Dance Theatre's acclaimed production of Bush.*

# Thrill City

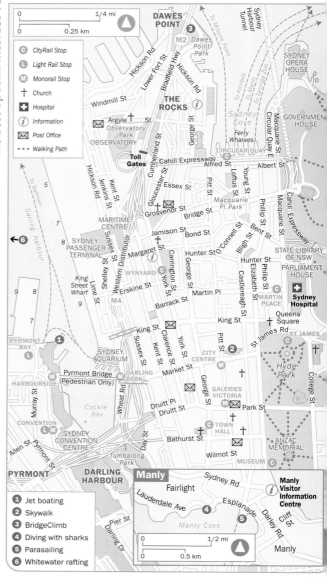

**Legend:**
- C CityRail Stop
- L Light Rail Stop
- M Monorail Stop
- + Church
- ✚ Hospital
- i Information
- ✉ Post Office
- ••• Walking Path

**1** Jet boating
**2** Skywalk
**3** BridgeClimb
**4** Diving with sharks
**5** Parasailing
**6** Whitewater rafting

**Manly**
Fairlight
Lauderdale Ave
Sydney Rd
Esplanade
Darley Rd
Cliff St
Manly Cove
Manly

i Manly Visitor Information Centre

Get ready to pump up the adrenalin in this thrill-seeker's guide to Sydney. From climbing the Coathanger and walking across the city skyline, to getting in over your head with man-eating sharks, this is a tour for those who like to spice up their day with a heart-pumping dose of adventure. START: **Monorail to Darling Harbour.**

*View to a thrill on Sydney Tower's Skywalk.*

**1** ★★ kids **Jet Boating.** A jet boat tour of Sydney Harbour is not a sightseeing tour. Sure, it's a harbor cruise (of sorts), but it's more about spins, wild fishtails, and power-brake stops that bury the nose of the boat. You *will* get wet. There are a number of jet boat companies that offer similar tours, but Harbour Jet is a winner. ⊕ 35–80 min. Convention Centre Jetty, Darling Harbour. ☎ 1300 887 373. www.harbourjet.com. Admission $65–$95 adults, $45–$70 kids (must be 130 cm/51 in. or taller). Several rides daily, see website for details. Monorail: Convention.

**2** ★ **Skywalk.** Check out the view from the 268m-high (879-ft.) glass-bottomed platform that hangs off the top of Sydney Tower. It's a thrill if you're nervous about heights, but others may find it a bit on the tame side for the price. Kids over 10 only. ⊕ 95 min. Corner Pitt & Market sts. ☎ 02/9333 9222. www.skywalk.com. au. Admission $65 adults, $45 kids, and includes entry to all other Sydney Tower attractions. See p 16, **8**.

**3** ★★★ **BridgeClimb.** See p 11, **8**.

**4** ★★★ **Diving with Sharks.** Oceanworld Manly runs adventure programs for both divers and nondivers where you get inside the tank and up close and personal with huge gray nurse sharks, giant stingrays, sea turtles, and other marine life. ⊕ 2½ hr. Admission $185–$350. See p 20, **8**.

**5** **Parasailing.** Get a bird's-eye view of Sydney Harbour as you're winched into the sky on a 150m (492-ft.) towline. Must be over 15. ⊕ 10 min. Manly Wharf. ☎ 02/9977 6781. www.parasail.net. Admission $85. Daily mid-Oct to early May. Ferry: Manly ferry from Circular Quay.

**6** **Whitewater Rafting.** Penrith Whitewater Stadium was the competition venue for the canoe/kayak slalom events during the 2000 Olympics. It's designed to re-create a wild river with 14,000 liters (3,698 gallons) of raging white water flowing per second over a moveable obstacle system. Must be over 12. ⊕ 90 min. McCarthy's Lane, Cranebrook. ☎ 02/4730 4333. www.penrithwhite water.com.au. Admission $89. Daily 9am–5pm. Train: Penrith (5 min. taxi ride from station).

# Food Safari

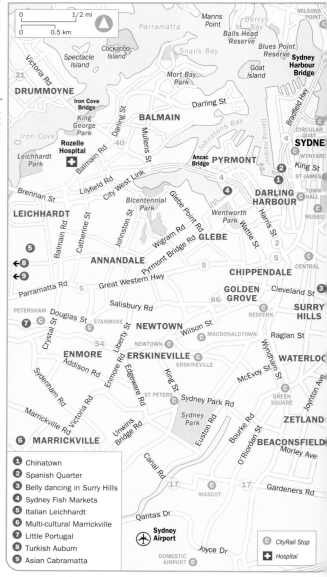

1. Chinatown
2. Spanish Quarter
3. Belly dancing in Surry Hills
4. Sydney Fish Markets
5. Italian Leichhardt
6. Multi-cultural Marrickville
7. Little Portugal
8. Turkish Auburn
9. Asian Cabramatta

🚉 CityRail Stop
✚ Hospital

**E**at your way around the world in multicultural Sydney. Who needs to leave town when you can get rich Italian espresso and gelato in Leichhardt, steaming bowls of pho in Vietnamese Cabramatta, or sweet Turkish Delight in Auburn? Take a food safari into Sydney's suburbs. START: **Take a train to Central and walk to Chinatown.**

*Fatima's restaurant in Surry Hills.*

**①** ★★★ **Chinatown.** Noodles, dim sum, yum cha, green tea, and cheap Chinoiserie. *See p 56.*

**②** **Spanish Quarter.** Not as big as it used to be since family-run restaurants are making way for new apartment buildings, the area between Liverpool and Kent streets

in the southern end of George Street is Sydney's Spanish Quarter, where tiny family-run restaurants dish out great paella, tapas, and jugs of ruby-red sangria. Best bet: Captain Torres. *73 Liverpool St.* ☎ *02/9264 5574. $$. Train: Town Hall.*

**③** ★ **Belly Dancing in Surry Hills.** Grab a floor cushion, tuck into a plate of just-cooked falafel and tangy tabbouleh, and sit back to watch some serious hip displacement at any one of the Lebanese restaurants and cafes along Cleveland Street. Best bet: Fatima's. (Belly dancing on Fri and Sat nights.) *294–296 Cleveland St.* ☎ *02/9698 4895. $$. Bus: 372, 393, 395.*

**④** ★★★ **Sydney Fish Markets.** It's the world's second largest seafood market, in terms of variety, outside of Japan and it auctions more than 100 species daily. Take an early morning, behind-the-scenes tour and catch the auction action, then breakfast (or lunch) on the freshest sushi and fish and chips in town. ⏱ *90*

*Fish market fare.*

*You'll find great coffee drinks in Leichhardt.*

*min. Bank St., Pyrmont. ☎ 02/9004 1143. www.sydneyfishmarket.com. au. Tours $20 adults, $10 kids 6–13. Market open daily from 7am. Tours depart 6:50am sharp Mon, Thurs, & Fri and you must wear enclosed shoes. Light rail: Fish Market.*

**⑤ ★★★ Italian Leichhardt.** This is the center of Sydney's Italian community. You'll find fantastic pasta and other Italian delicacies for sale in the string of delis and food stores along Norton Street, along with the best coffee and gelato this side of Palermo. Best bet: Bar Italia. Locals line up on the footpath for a table or a big cone of gelato. Try the iced coffee. *169 Norton St. ☎ 02/9560 9981. $. Bus: 440.*

**⑥ Multicultural Marrickville.** Once upon a time this working-class suburb was the heart of the Australian Greek community, but in the past decade or so it's become more Vietnamese. Either way, eating out is cheap, cheerful, and definitely a family affair. Illawarra Road is lined with family-run restaurants of both culinary persuasions. Best bet: Pho Ha Noi Quan. *346b Illawarra Rd. ☎ 02/9559 1637. $. Train: Marrickville.*

**⑦ ★★ Little Portugal.** If you've got a hankering for the best custard tarts in Sydney, head to Petersham, otherwise known as Little Portugal, where you'll find much more than Portuguese chicken. Best bet: La Patisserie. Pastries so fine you'll think you've gone to cake heaven. *45 New Canterbury Rd. ☎ 02/9569 1107. $. Train: Petersham.*

**⑧ Turkish Auburn.** Head west, young man (or woman), for the city's finest Turkish delight, thickest Turkish coffee, and sweetest apple tea—and try to resist picking up a carpet or two while you're there. Best bet: Mado Café. Wild orchid ice cream so thick you need a knife and fork (same could be said about the coffee). *63 Auburn Rd. ☎ 02/9643 5299. $$. Train: Auburn.*

**⑨ ★★★ Asian Cabramatta.** Spending a day in the Asian food capital of Sydney is like taking a day trip to Asia, complete with all the requisite sights, sounds, and smells— about as far away from WASP Sydney as you can get. Shop the market, buy some bargain fabrics, visit an herbalist, slurp some pho. Best bet: Pho 54. It's all about the divine noodle soup. *54 Park Rd. ☎ 02/9726 1992. $. Train: Cabramatta.* ●

## Gourmet Safari

Get the inside story, meet the cooks and chefs, and taste the local delicacies on a guided full-day tour of some of Sydney's best eating and cultural enclaves with celebrity TV foodie, **Maeve O'Meara** (☎ **02/8969 6555;** www.gourmetsafaris.com.au). Tours cost $115 to $140.

# The Rocks

The Best Neighborhood Walks

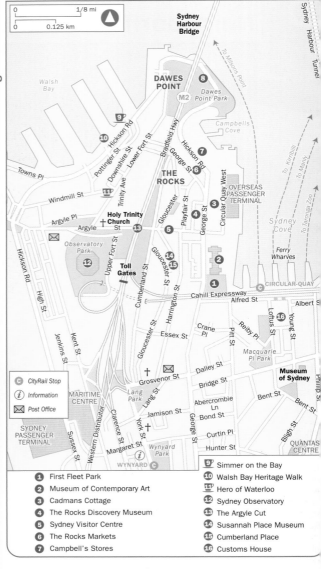

1 First Fleet Park
2 Museum of Contemporary Art
3 Cadmans Cottage
4 The Rocks Discovery Museum
5 Sydney Visitor Centre
6 The Rocks Markets
7 Campbell's Stores
9 Simmer on the Bay
10 Walsh Bay Heritage Walk
11 Hero of Waterloo
12 Sydney Observatory
13 The Argyle Cut
14 Susannah Place Museum
15 Cumberland Place
16 Customs House

*Previous page: The tram at Darling Harbor.*

Named for the sandstone cliffs that the area was built upon and carved into, The Rocks is Sydney's most historic suburb—with a colorful past. Until the late 20th century, when it became a gentrified tourist destination full of museums, galleries, and boutiques, The Rocks was a hotbed of vice. It was originally an open-air jail in the first days of the convict colony before becoming renowned in the late 19th century for its drunken debauchery, sailors, brothels, and generally unsavory characters; it was known as an overcrowded slum in the early 20th century. START: **Train to Circular Quay.**

**1** **First Fleet Park.** There are usually a few buskers—expect anything from amplified didgeridoos to human statues and acrobats—enlivening this busy city park with great views across to the Opera House. ⏱ *10 min. George St.*

**2** ★ **Museum of Contemporary Art.** See p 27, **2**.

**3** **Cadmans Cottage.** Built in 1816, this two-story simple cottage is one of the oldest buildings in the city. It housed the government coxswain, the man responsible for government boats and their crews in the early days of the colony. It originally stood just meters from the harbor's edge, before sea walls were built enabling land reclamation. It's now the information center for Sydney Harbour National Park. ⏱ *10 min. 110 George St. North.* ☎ *02/9253 0888. Free admission. Mon–Fri 9:30am–4:30pm; Sat–Sun 10am–4:30pm.*

**4** ★★ 🄺🄸🄳🅂 **The Rocks Discovery Museum.** Housed in a restored 1850s sandstone warehouse, this modern museum focuses just on The Rocks. Its displays relate to the traditional owners (the Cadigal people), the establishment of the colony, and various other aspects of life in The Rocks over the past 220 years—from the outbreak of the bubonic plague in 1900 and widespread demolition to make way for the Harbour Bridge in the 1930s, to the

*Cadmans Cottage.*

"green bans" ecoactivism of the 1970s. Great collection of artifacts found in archaeological digs and some terrific archival film footage. ⏱ *45 min. Kendall Lane (off Argyle St.).* ☎ *02/9251 8804. www.rocks discoverymuseum.com. Free admission. Daily 10am–5pm.*

**5** **Sydney Visitor Centre.** Pick up free maps and anything else you need to know about the city. ⏱ *10 min. Corner Argyle & Playfair sts.* ☎ *02/9240 8788. www.sydney visitorcentre.com. Daily 9:30am–5:30pm.*

**6** ★ **The Rocks Markets.** There is some tourist tat, but most of the art, crafts, jewelry, and homewares on sale here is good quality. ⏱ *1 hr. Northern end of George St. Sat–Sun 10am–5pm.*

**7 Campbell's Stores.** These 11 gable-fronted, three-story warehouses were built by the "merchant prince" of the colony, Robert Campbell, between 1839 and 1861 and once housed everything from tea to liquor. Not that much has changed really since today they are home to restaurants and bars. 🕐 *10 min. 7–27 Circular Quay West. Free admission.*

**8 Dawes Point (Tar-ra).** Take a walk under the arches of the Harbour Bridge alongside Hickson Road and admire the view across to North Sydney.

A great waterfront spot for a casual bite to eat is **9 Simmer on the Bay.** The gourmet sandwiches are the size of a brick, and on weekends you can laze back in a deck chair as you soak in the view. *Between piers 2/3 & 4/5.* ☎ *02/9247 2457. $.*

**10 Walsh Bay Heritage Walk.** Take a self-guided tour around the heritage finger wharves of Walsh Bay on the western side of The Rocks. Storyboards and artifacts on display tell the story of the area and the people who worked and lived there. Juxtaposed against all this gritty industrial heritage is a modern sculpture trail with supersize bright art installations from some of Australia's best known artists, including Brett Whiteley. 🕐 *30 min. Hickson St.*

*Art installations at Walsh Bay.*

One of my favorite things is to **11 pop into one of the dozen or so historic pubs for a cold drink.** A good choice is the Hero of Waterloo, built in 1842. Rumor has it that there are secret tunnels that connect the pub to the harbor in order to shanghai unfortunate drinkers onto ships. A band usually performs on Sunday afternoons. *81 Lower Fort St.* ☎ *02/9252 4553. $.*

**12 ★ kids Sydney Observatory.** Built in 1858, Australia's oldest observatory was a working one until the 1970s when increasing light pollution made observations too difficult—it is now a museum. Highlights include the Cadi Eora Birrung exhibit, which looks at Sydney's stars from an Aboriginal perspective, and the Transit of Venus, which was one of the main reasons why Cook set sail to the other side of the world, discovering Australia after observing the transit in Tahiti back in 1769. 🕐 *45 min. Watson Rd., Observatory Hill.* ☎ *02/9921 3485. www.sydney observatory.com.au. Free admission. Nighttime stargazing tours daily (bookings essential), $17 adults, $10 kids. Daily 10am–5pm.*

**13 The Argyle Cut.** This tunnel through the sandstone ridge connects The Rocks to Millers Point and Darling Harbour and was one of the most impressive engineering feats in

*Birds-eye view of the model city at the Customs House.*

early Sydney. Work began in 1843 with convicts in chain gangs and was finally completed using explosives in 1859. ⏱ *10 min. Argyle St. (Cambridge St. through to Bradfield Hwy.).*

**⑭ ★★★ Susannah Place Museum.** Most museums preserve and tell the story of grand houses or institutions. Not this one. This row of four tiny terrace houses and a corner shop was built in 1844 and was home to more than 100 families over 150 years, right up until 1990—quite astounding given the primitive and cramped conditions. The 1-hour guided tour, coupled with oral histories, illustrates the life and times of the tenants, who, despite outsiders deriding the area as a "slum worse than London" and the government pursuing a strategy of "demolition by neglect," were proud of their homes and treasured the tightknit working-class community around them. ⏱ *1 hr. 58–64 Gloucester St. ☎ 02/9241 1893. www.hht.net.au. Admission $8 adults, $4 kids. Mon–Fri 2–6pm; Sat–Sun 10am–6pm (5pm June–Aug).*

**⑮ Cumberland Place.** This network of narrow streets and steps worn concave by the passing of countless feet dates back to before 1807. ⏱ *10 min. Opposite Susannah Place Museum, Gloucester St.*

**⑯ Customs House.** Built in 1845 and headquarters of the Customs Service until 1990, the City of Sydney Library is on the first floor (check out the model of Sydney under your feet and take advantage of free Wi-Fi) and a very fine restaurant, Cafe Sydney (p 98), is on the rooftop. ⏱ *10 min. 31 Alfred St. ☎ 02/9242 8595. Free admission. Library open Mon–Fri 10am–7pm; Sat–Sun 11am–4pm; closed public holidays.*

## Ghosts & Ghouls

If an evening of murder, mayhem, suicides, hangings, and grisly violent crime sounds like your kind of thing, join a **Rocks Ghost Tour** (☎ 02/9247 7910; www.ghosttours.com.au) and explore a different side of Sydney on this excellent 2-hour walking tour. The cost is $42; tours are available daily 6:45pm April to September, 7:45pm October to March. Bookings are essential.

# Chinatown & Darling Harbour

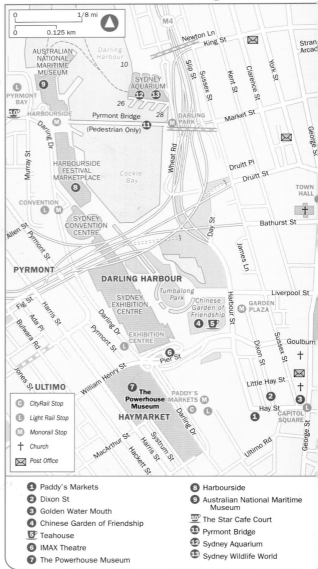

1. Paddy's Markets
2. Dixon St
3. Golden Water Mouth
4. Chinese Garden of Friendship
5. Teahouse
6. IMAX Theatre
7. The Powerhouse Museum
8. Harbourside
9. Australian National Maritime Museum
10. The Star Cafe Court
11. Pyrmont Bridge
12. Sydney Aquarium
13. Sydney Wildlife World

Chinatown's great food, bargains, and Asian vibe speak for themselves, but it can be tempting to dismiss Darling Harbour as just for kids. Take a closer look, however, and you'll find there is plenty to keep grown-ups amused in these once-derelict docklands. A lot of Sydneysiders will tell you it's a tourist ghetto and not worth the effort, but come sundown you'll find they flock to the many restaurants, bars, and nightclubs here. START: **Monorail to Paddy's Markets or walk from Central Station.**

*Drummers in Chinatown, Chinese New Year.*

**1 Paddy's Markets.** The market has been here since 1834, although back then it was all about hay, grain, and cattle—hence the neighborhood name: Haymarket. These days there are close to 1,000 stalls that sell everything from fresh produce to fashion, accessories, electrical goods, and souvenirs. ⏱ *1 hr. Hay St. Free admission. Wed–Sun 9am–5pm.*

**2 ★★★ Dixon Street.** Chinatown began life as a cluster of Chinese market gardeners and traders at the turn of last century, and it's now a thriving cultural community where you can buy all sorts of Chinese goods, foods, and herbal medicines. Chinatown covers several city blocks in the Haymarket area and west to Darling Harbour, but the heart and soul is Dixon Street. At each end you'll find ceremonial Chinese gates, and the pedestrian-only street features distinctly oriental architecture, street lanterns, and archways. It's lined with Chinese shophouses and restaurants, many open very late. ⏱ *1 hr.*

**3 Golden Water Mouth.** The five natural elements (gold, water, wood, fire, and earth) in this arresting 10m-high (33-ft.) sculpture made from a dead tree trunk are meant to bring good fortune and promote positive energy. Going by the buzz in nearby Dixon Street, I'd say it works. ⏱ *5 min. Corner George & Hay sts.*

**4 ★★ kids Chinese Garden of Friendship.** This lovely 1-hectare (2½-acre) traditional Chinese garden was opened to celebrate the

# Chinese New Year

Sydney's Chinese New Year Festival (late Jan to early Feb) is the largest Lunar New Year celebration outside Asia. There are more than 50 events over 3 weeks, with dragon boat races, acrobats, parades, markets, music, drums, dance, and costumes, culminating in an explosion of traditional Chinese firecrackers to scare away evil spirits and ensure prosperity for the coming year.

bicentennial in 1988 and is meant to be a symbol of the friendship between Sydney and its sister city Guangzhou in Guangdong Province, China. Favorite spots include the moon gate, the pagoda overlooking the lake and waterfall, the *penjing* (bonsai) garden, and the exquisite bridal carriage made from 300 tons of raw jade. Kids love dressing up and having their photo taken in the princess and warrior costumes. ⏱ *30 min. Southern end of Darling Harbour.* ☎ *02/9240 8888. www.chinesegarden.com.au. Admission $6 adults, $3 kids. Daily 9:30am–5pm.*

Contemplate the spirit of friendship with a cup of Old Man's Eyebrows (otherwise known as Shou Mei, it's a

light green tea). Enjoy your cup in the **5** **teahouse inside the Chinese Garden of Friendship.** You can also get English-style teas here as well as dim sim, gow gee dumplings, steamed pork buns, and sandwiches. *In the Chinese Garden of Friendship. 02/9240 8888. $.*

**6** kids **IMAX Theatre.** See p 127.

**7** ★★★ kids **Powerhouse Museum.** See p 40, **5**.

**8** **Harbourside.** There are two levels of specialty shops in this waterfront shopping center, though it does tend to attract mainly tourists.

**9** ★★★ kids **Australian National Maritime Museum.** Those big boats moored on the

*Artwork in the Chinese Garden of Friendship.*

*Pyrmont Bridge.*

western side of Darling Harbour—the massive destroyer HMAS *Vampire,* among the largest big gun destroyers built in Australia; the submarine HMAS *Onslow;* the attack-class patrol boat; and the colorful replica of the *Endeavour,* the tiny sailing ship in which Cook discovered Australia—all belong to the Australian Maritime Museum. Inside the museum you'll find all sorts of displays relating to Australia's maritime heritage, from commerce to navigation and the history of the bathing suit, as well as traveling exhibitions—but it's the amazing collection moored at the adjacent wharf that is really something. All the ships are open for tours. 🕐 *1–2 hr. Murray St.* 📞 *02/9298 3777. www.anmm.gov.au. Museum free admission. Big Ticket $32 adults, $17 kids, $70 family (includes entry to HM Bark Endeavour replica, destroyer HMAS Vampire, submarine HMAS Onslow, and the 1874 tall ship James Craig). Daily 9:30am–5pm (6pm in Jan).*

Don't be put off that 🔟 **the Star Café Court** is part of the casino. Enter by Pyrmont Street and you

won't even see the gaming area. Many of Sydney's celebrity chefs have outlets here serving their food at half the price you'd pay in their restaurants. Try the dumplings at Din Tai Fung or fish and chips at Flying Fish, and finish off with artisan gelato at Messina or a sweet treat at Adriano Zumbo. *80 Pyrmont St. $.*

**⑪ Pyrmont Bridge.** Built in 1902, this is the oldest surviving electrical swing bridge in the world. Powered by electricity, it can swing open and shut in 45 seconds and is still operating. You can see it in action on Saturdays, Sundays, and most public holidays at 10:30am, noon, 1pm, 2pm, and 3pm (weather permitting). It is also opened as required for shipping. Tours are available. 🕐 *10 min.* 📞 *02/9299 7541. Free admission. Tour bookings essential. Monorail: Harbourside.*

**⑫ ★★★ kids Sydney Aquarium.** *See p 39,* ❷.

**⑬ ★★ kids Sydney Wildlife World.** *See p 39,* ❸.

# Surry Hills

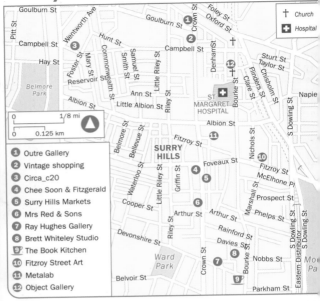

**Map legend:**

† Church
➕ Hospital

Goulburn St · Pitt St · Campbell St · Hay St · Belmore Park · Wentworth Ave · Hunt St · Foster St · Mary St · Commonwealth St · Reservoir St · Samuel St · Smith St · Ann St · Little Albion St · Little Riley St · Riley St · Albion St · Goulburn St · Crown St · Foley St · Oxford St · Campbell St · Denham St · Sturt St · Taylor St · Chisholm St · Flinders St · Clare St · Bourke St · ST MARGARET HOSPITAL · Albion St · S Dowling St · Napie · Fitzroy St · Belmore St · Bellevue St · SURRY HILLS · Nichols St · Foveaux St · Fitzroy St · McElhone Pl · Waterloo St · Little Riley St · Griffin St · Prospect St · Marshall St · Cooper St · Arthur St · Arthur St · Phelps St · Riley St · Rainford St · Davies St · S Dowling St · Devonshire St · Crown St · Nobbs St · Bourke St · Eastern Distributor · S Dowling St · Mo Pa · Ward Park · Belvoir St · Parkham St

0 — 1/8 mi
0 — 0.125 km

1. Outre Gallery
2. Vintage shopping
3. Circa_c20
4. Chee Soon & Fitzgerald
5. Surry Hills Markets
6. Mrs Red & Sons
7. Ray Hughes Gallery
8. Brett Whiteley Studio
9. The Book Kitchen
10. Fitzroy Street Art
11. Metalab
12. Object Gallery

I f Charles Dickens had written a novel about Sydney, it would have been set in Surry Hills. One hundred years ago it was an overcrowded inner-city slum, notorious for its brothels, gangs, and street urchins. Now it's a vibrant corner of the city, packed with 🐖 galleries and boutiques full of supercool streetwear, quirky gifts, cutting-edge design, and some of the best value restaurants in town.
START: **Bus 378 or 380 to corner of Oxford and Crown streets.**

**①  Outre Gallery.** Half shop, half gallery space. If you are into pop art, counterculture, and graphic design you'll love this place, which has the best contemporary pop art in the city with everything from original artwork to ceramics and vinyl toys. Exhibitions change monthly. *Shop 7, 285A Crown St. ☎ 02/9332 2776. www. outregallery.com. Mon–Wed 11am–6pm; Thurs 11am–8pm; Fri 11am–6pm; Sat 10am–5pm; Sun noon–4pm*

*Tea set and glassware at Circa.*

**2 Vintage Shopping.** From high-end rockabilly to cheap chic and vintage lingerie, the Oxford Street end of Crown Street has an ever-changing collection of vintage-inspired clothing and accessory shops. ⏰ 45 min.

**3 Circa_c20.** Twentieth-century collectibles with a focus on ceramics and glass. ⏰ 15 min. Sydney Antique Centre, 531 South Dowling St. ☎ 02/9361 3244. www.circa-c20.com.au. Tues–Fri 11am–6pm (10am–4pm in winter); Sat 11am–4pm.

**4 ★★ Chee Soon & Fitzgerald.** A limited edition hand-printed tea towel from here makes a perfect souvenir. ⏰ 15 min. 387 Crown St. ☎ 02/9360 1031. Daily 10am–6pm.

**5 ★★ Surry Hills Markets.** It's all secondhand and handmade at this monthly market in the park. ⏰ 45 min. Corner Crown & Collins sts. First Sat of the month.

**6 ★★★ Mrs. Red & Sons.** Behind the intriguing red door is a fabulous collection of Asian desirables. ⏰ 15 min. 427 Crown St. ☎ 02/9310 4860. Tues–Fri 11am–6pm; Sat 10am–5pm; Sun noon–4pm.

**7 ★★ Ray Hughes Gallery.** One of the city's best private

Asian treasures await behind the signature red door at Mrs. Red & Sons.

contemporary art galleries with changing exhibitions. ⏰ 20 min. 270 Devonshire St. ☎ 02/9698 3200. Tues–Sat 10am–6pm.

**8 ★★★ Brett Whiteley Studio.** See p 28, **9**.

New and used books for food lovers and very good organic food at **9' the Book Kitchen.** Be prepared to wait for a table on weekends. 255 Devonshire St. ☎ 02/9310 1003. $–$$.

**10 Fitzroy Street Art.** Taking street art off the streets and hanging it on the walls, this gallery features the work of up-and-coming street artists in a program of changing exhibitions as well as iconic images from artists like Banksy and Shepard Fairey (of Obama poster fame). ⏰ 20 min. 90 Fitzroy St., Surry Hills. ☎ 02/9331 6614. Daily 11am–5:30pm.

**11 Metalab.** One-off jewelry and design from local and international artists. ⏰ 15 min. 10b Fitzroy Place. ☎ 02/8354 1398. Wed–Sat 11am–6pm.

**12 ★★ Object Gallery.** ⏰ 30 min. See p 29, **10**.

A gallery on Fitzroy Street.

# Glebe & Newtown

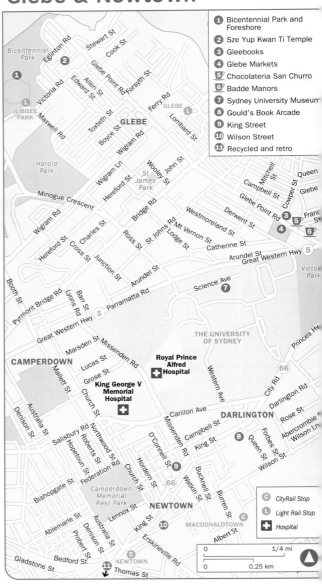

1. Bicentennial Park and Foreshore
2. Sze Yup Kwan Ti Temple
3. Gleebooks
4. Glebe Markets
5. Chocolateria San Churro
6. Badde Manors
7. Sydney University Museum
8. Gould's Book Arcade
9. King Street
10. Wilson Street
11. Recycled and retro

**C** CityRail Stop
**L** Light Rail Stop
**+** Hospital

| 0 | | 1/4 mi |
| 0 | 0.25 km | |

Glebe and Newtown is Sydney's urban street culture at its best. It's gritty and not always pretty, but with the University of Sydney at its heart, this area is a bohemian mix of students, artists, intellectuals, activists, Goths, gays, and anyone else drawn to the unconventional buzz of streets packed with cafes, bars, secondhand book and music shops, galleries, tiny theaters, retro and recycled fashion, and furniture. START: **Light Rail to Glebe, or bus 431 or 433 to corner of Glebe Point Road and Ferry Road.**

*The angels of the coffee machine at Badde Manors.*

**1** ★★ **Bicentennial Park.** From the end of Ferry Road take a walk around the foreshore of Glebe Point and enjoy the views of the stunning Anzac Bridge, the longest cable-stayed bridge in Australia. ⏲ *30 min.*

**2** ★ **Sze Yup Kwan Ti Temple.** Built in 1898, this Chinese temple hidden away in the back streets is dedicated to Kwan Ti, a warrior god. ⏲ *15 min. 2 Edward St. Daily 9am–5pm. Free admission.*

**3** ★★★ **Gleebooks.** The best of the Glebe Point Road bookstores that sell both new and secondhand books. ⏲ *15 min. 49 Glebe Point Rd. ☎ 02 /9660 2333. www.gleebooks.com.au. Daily 9am–9pm. Bus: 431, 433.*

**4** ★★★ **kids Glebe Markets.** Every Saturday the public school grounds are home to one of the best alternative markets in the city, with lots of preloved clothes, secondhand books, music, and slightly out-there arts and crafts. A big grassy area is great for kids to run around on, and there's usually some entertainment. ⏲ *45 min. Glebe Primary School, Glebe Point Rd. Sat 10am–4pm. Bus: 431, 433.*

Get your chocolate fix at **5** **Chocolateria San Churro** with delicious churros—Spanish fried dough—dipped in liquid chocolate. Yum! *47 Glebe Point Rd. ☎ 02/9692 0119. $.*

Despite its languid service, **6** ★★ **Badde Manors** is a Glebe institution. The food's pretty good, but it's mainly about soaking up the classic coffeehouse atmosphere and eclectic decor. *1/37 Glebe Point Rd. ☎ 02/9660 3797. $.*

**7** ★★★ **Sydney University Museums.** Founded in 1850, Australia's oldest university is a stunning example of Gothic Revival architecture—the beautiful quadrangle with its monastic cloisters in particular. There are three museums around the quadrangle and all are free. The University Art Gallery is small and has a program of changing exhibits; the Macleay Museum favors the scientific and is home to the amazing collection of insects assembled by Alexander Macleay (of Elizabeth House fame); the Nicholson Museum is home to the largest collection of antiquities in Australia, including Egyptian mummies. If you're visiting in early spring, duck into the delightfully secret Vice Chancellor's Garden in the northwest corner of the quad when the azaleas and camellias are in full bloom. 🕐 90 min. Off University Ave. ☎ 02/9351 2222. www.sydney.edu.au/museums. Mon–Fri 10am–4:30pm; Sun noon–4pm. Bus: 412, 413, 435, 438, 440, 461, 480, 483.

**8 ★★★ Gould's Book Arcade.** A cavernous temple to secondhand and out-of-print books that covers just about anything and everything, although the Australian history, politics, and art sections are huge. 🕐 20 min. 32 King St. ☎ 02/9519 8947. Daily 10am–10pm. Train: Newtown.

*Newtown street art.*

**9 ★★★ King Street.** A stroll down King Street toward Newtown Station is not so much about places as people. The streetscape is a great example of 19th-century commercial architecture and includes a range of styles from high Victorian Gothic to Queen Anne Revival and Italianate. The eastern end (closer to Sydney University) is slightly more gentrified, but still graffiti-strewn. There are plenty of funky streetwear shops, art galleries, and cheap cafes for people-watching. Reiki and iridology centers sit beside organic cafes and adult book stores, and it gets increasingly more unconventional further west down King Street. 🕐 2 hr.

**10 ★★ Wilson Street.** Duck up Wilson Street for secondhand and independent music at Egg Records and vintage posters at Blue Dog. They're proudly "Keeping Newtown Weird." *Egg Records: 3 Wilson St. ☎ 02/9550 6056. Mon–Sat 10am–6:30pm; Thurs 10am–7pm; Sun 11am–5pm. Blue Dog Posters & Prints: 9 Wilson St. ☎ 02/1300 781 002. Mon–Fri 10am–6pm; Sat 10am–5pm; Sun noon–5pm.*

**11 ★★★ Recycled and Retro.** West of Newtown Station, secondhand clothing and houseware shops predominate. Best bargain bets include Repressed Records for secondhand CDs and vinyl, All Buttons Great and Small for an extravagant collection of buttons, and Newtown Old Wares for "deco to disco" stuff. 🕐 30–60 min. *Repressed Records: 356 King St. ☎ 02/9557 6237. Mon–Wed 11am–7pm; Thurs 10am–8:30pm; Fri–Sat 10am–7pm; Sun 11am–6pm. All Buttons Great and Small: 419a King St. ☎ 02/9550 1782. Mon–Wed 10am–5pm; Thurs 10am–7pm; Fri 10am–5pm; Sat 10am–4pm. Newtown Old Wares: 439 King St. ☎ 02/9519 6705. Tues–Sat 10am–5pm; Sun 11am–4pm.* ●

# Shopping **Best Bets**

Best **Beachwear**
★★ Billabong, *Sydney Arcade,*
*Pitt Street Mall (p 73)*

Most Beautiful **Place to Shop**
★★★ Queen Victoria Building,
*George St. (p 71)*

Best **Books**
★★★ Gleebooks, *49 Glebe Point Rd.*
*(p 74)*

Best **Department Store**
★★ David Jones, *65 Market St. &*
*86 Castlereagh St. (p 74)*

Best **Designer Denim**
Ksubi, *82 Gould St. (p 73)*

Best **Local Market**
★★★ Bondi Markets, *Campbell*
*Parade (p 75)*

Best **PJs**
★★★ Peter Alexander, *Pitt Street*
*Mall (p 76)*

Best **Time to Shop**
Boxing Day (Dec 26) through to
the end of January, and late June
to mid-July, for citywide sales

Best **Place for Unique Gifts**
★★★ Collect, *417 Bourke St. (p 71)*

Best **Vintage**
★★★ Coco Repose, *Sydney*
*Antiques Centre, 531 South Dowling*
*St. (p 76)*

## Nontouristy Touristy Souvenirs

Don't leave Sydney without a couple of coat hangers in your
luggage. The **Sydney Visitor Centre,** on the corner of Argyle and
Playfair streets in The Rocks
(☎ **02/9240 8788;** www.sydney
visitorcentre.com), stocks my
favorite Sydney souvenir—
Harbour Bridge (aka "the Coat
Hanger") clothes hangers. You
can't get more Sydney than that!
They also have some natty little
trays for your freezer that make
ice cubes in the shape of Australia
or koalas (pictured), so every time
you enjoy a cold drink you'll think
of summer in Sydney.

*Australia ice cubes.*

# Oxford Street & Bondi Shopping

Akira 11
Alannah Hill 2
Alistair Trung 10
Berkelouw Books 1
Bikini Island 15
Bondi Markets 18
Collette
  Dinnigan 13
Di Nuovo 8
Dinosaur Designs 4
Easton Pearson 9

Grandma Takes
  a Trip 17
Ksubi 16
Lisa Ho 12
Mr Rose 9
Paddington
  Markets 8
Pelle 5
Sass & Bide 3
Westfield Bondi
  Junction (WBJ) 14

# Inner Sydney Shopping

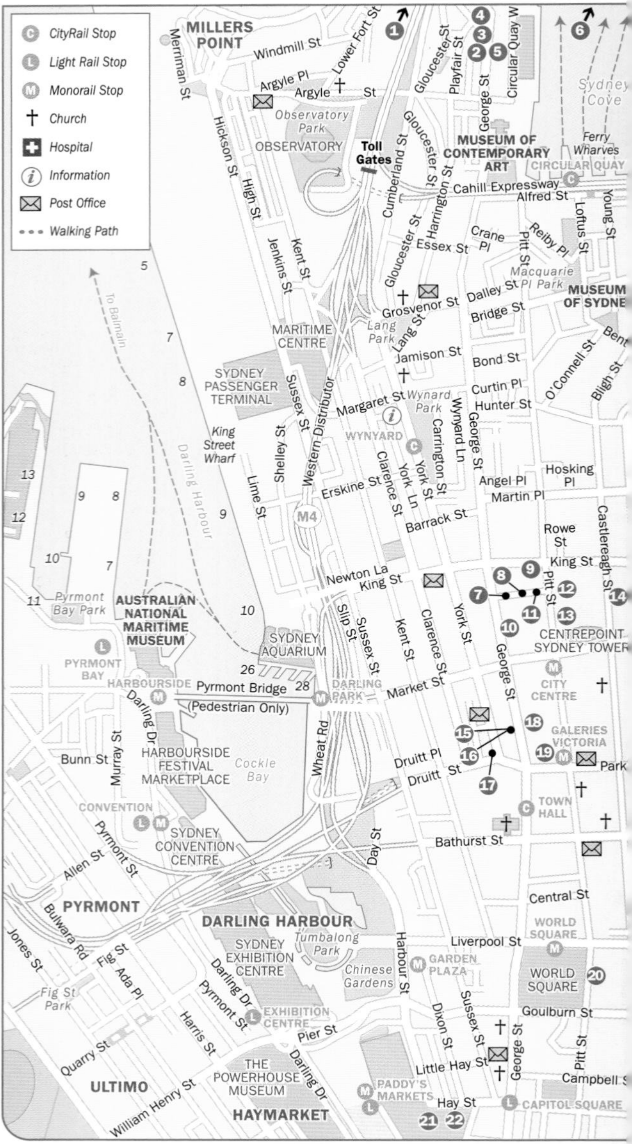
CityRail Stop
Light Rail Stop
Monorail Stop
Church
Hospital
Information
Post Office
Walking Path
MILLERS POINT
Windmill St
Argyle Pl
Argyle St
Lower Fort St
Observatory Park
OBSERVATORY
Toll Gates
Hickson St
High St
Kent St
Jenkins St
Merriman St
Gloucester St
Playfair St
George St
Circular Quay W
Sydney Cove
Ferry Wharves
MUSEUM OF CONTEMPORARY ART
CIRCULAR QUAY
Cahill Expressway
Alfred St
Cumberland St
Harrington St
Essex St
Crane Pl
Pitt St
Reiby Pl
Loftus St
Young St
Macquarie Pl Park
MUSEUM OF SYDNEY
Dalley St
Bridge St
Grosvenor St
Lang Park
Lang St
Jamison St
Bond St
Curtin Pl
Hunter St
O'Connell St
Bligh St
MARITIME CENTRE
SYDNEY PASSENGER TERMINAL
To Balmain
King Street Wharf
Sussex St
Western Distributor
Margaret St
Wynyard Park
WYNYARD
Carrington St
Wynyard Ln
Shelley St
Lime St
Darling Harbour
Clarence St
York Ln
York St
Erskine St
Barrack St
Angel Pl
Martin Pl
Hosking Pl
Rowe St
Castlereagh St
King St
M4
Newton La
Pyrmont Bay Park
AUSTRALIAN NATIONAL MARITIME MUSEUM
SYDNEY AQUARIUM
Slip St
CENTREPOINT SYDNEY TOWER
PYRMONT BAY
HARBOURSIDE
Pyrmont Bridge (Pedestrian Only)
DARLING PARK
Market St
CITY CENTRE
Darling Dr
GALERIES VICTORIA
Park
Bunn St
Murray St
HARBOURSIDE FESTIVAL MARKETPLACE
Cockle Bay
Wheat Rd
Druitt Pl
Druitt St
CONVENTION
TOWN HALL
SYDNEY CONVENTION CENTRE
Pyrmont St
Allen St
Day St
Bathurst St
PYRMONT
Central St
DARLING HARBOUR
Bulwara Rd
Jones St
Fig St
Ada Pl
SYDNEY EXHIBITION CENTRE
Tumbalong Park
Chinese Gardens
Harbour St
Liverpool St
WORLD SQUARE
GARDEN PLAZA
Fig St Park
Harris St
EXHIBITION CENTRE
Dixon St
Goulburn St
Quarry St
Pier St
THE POWERHOUSE MUSEUM
Little Hay St
ULTIMO
PADDY'S MARKETS
Hay St
CAPITOL SQUARE
Campbell St
William Henry St
HAYMARKET

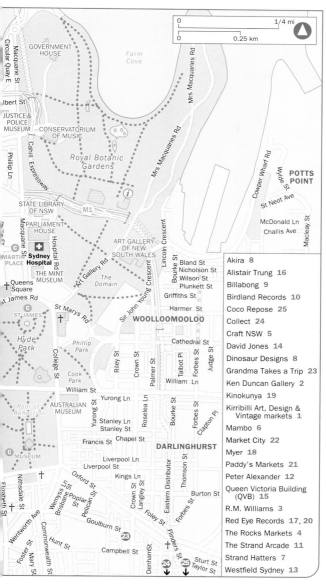

Akira 8
Alistair Trung 16
Billabong 9
Birdland Records 10
Coco Repose 25
Collect 24
Craft NSW 5
David Jones 14
Dinosaur Designs 8
Grandma Takes a Trip 23
Ken Duncan Gallery 2
Kinokunya 19
Kirribilli Art, Design &
  Vintage markets 1
Mambo 6
Market City 22
Myer 18
Paddy's Markets 21
Peter Alexander 12
Queen Victoria Building
  (QVB) 15
R.M. Williams 3
Red Eye Records 17, 20
The Rocks Markets 4
The Strand Arcade 11
Strand Hatters 7
Westfield Sydney 13

# Glebe & Newtown Shopping

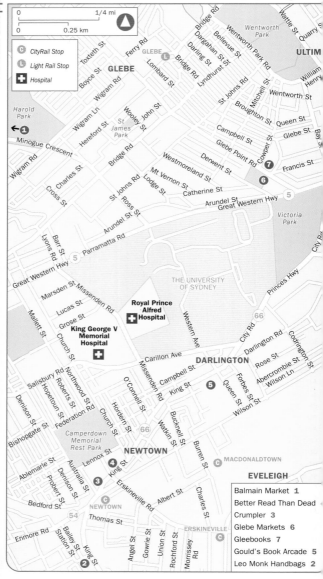

0 | 1/4 mi
0 | 0.25 km

**C** CityRail Stop
**L** Light Rail Stop
**+** Hospital

Harold Park

Minogue Crescent

GLEBE

ULTIM

Wentworth Park

St James Park

Victoria Park

THE UNIVERSITY OF SYDNEY

Royal Prince Alfred Hospital

King George V Memorial Hospital

DARLINGTON

Camperdown Memorial Rest Park

NEWTOWN

MACDONALDTOWN

ERSKINEVILLE

EVELEIGH

| Balmain Market | 1 |
| Better Read Than Dead | |
| Crumpler | 3 |
| Glebe Markets | 6 |
| Gleebooks | 7 |
| Gould's Book Arcade | 5 |
| Leo Monk Handbags | 2 |

# Sydney **Shopping A to Z**

**Arcades & Shopping Centers**
### ★★★ Queen Victoria Building
**(QVB)** CITY CENTER  Built in 1898, this building has flamboyant architectural details that include stained glass windows, intricate mosaic floors, and two large mechanical clocks, each one featuring dioramas and moving figures from moments in Australian history. Oh, and 200 shops. The statue of Queen Victoria at the town hall entrance originally stood outside the Irish Houses of Parliament in Dublin. *George St. (btw. Park & Market sts.). www.qvb. com.au. Train: Town Hall. Map p 68.*

### ★★★ The Strand Arcade CITY
CENTER  The only surviving grand Victorian-era arcade, the Strand was built in 1891 and is just as elegant now as it was back then. Today it's home to a cluster of some of Australia's top designer labels. History buffs will appreciate that it was one of the first places in the city to be lit by electricity. *412 George St. (through to Pitt Street Mall). www. strandarcade.com.au. Train: Martin Place. Map p 68.*

### ★★★ WBJ BONDI JUNCTION
Along with the usual suspects, WBJ is home to some big-name designers like Versace and Bally as well as home-grown talent such as Peter Alexander, Wayne Cooper, and Leona Edmiston. With more than 400 specialty stores and a number of department stores, if you can't spend money here you're just not trying. *500 Oxford St. www.west field.com/bondijunction. Train: Bondi Junction. Map p 67.*

**Westfield Sydney** CITY CENTER Like its Bondi cousin, this huge shopping complex has a mix of top Australian designers and international high street fashion. It also has

*The Strand Arcade.*

some surprisingly fine dining on the upper levels. *188 Pitt St. (Pitt Street Mall). www.westfield.com.au/sydney. Train: Martin Place. Map p 68.*

**Art, Craft & Design**
### ★★★ Collect SURRY HILLS  The
retail arm of the not-for-profit Object Gallery with unique ceramics, collectible glass, homewares, and jewelry. *417 Bourke St. ☎ 02/9361 4511. www.object.com.au. AE, MC, V. Bus: 378, 380. Map p 68.*

### ★★★ Craft NSW THE ROCKS
Original, high-quality Australian handicrafts—decorative and functional— in the old Coroner's Court. *104 George St. ☎ 02/9241 5825. AE, MC, V. Train: Circular Quay. Map p 68.*

### ★ Dinosaur Designs CITY CEN-
TER & PADDINGTON  Another Paddington Market success story, these bright and colorful homewares and chunky jewelry are handmade from resin and are very, very covetable. *Shop 77, Strand Arcade. ☎ 02/9223 2953. Train: Martin Place. 339 Oxford*

*The collection at Collect.*

St. ☎ 02/9361 3776. Bus: 380, 378. AE, MC, V. Map p 67 and 68.

### Australiana

**Ken Duncan Gallery** THE ROCKS Stunning limited edition large-format panoramic photographs of Australian landscapes. *73 George St.* ☎ 02/9241 3460. AE, DC, MC, V. Train: Circular Quay. Map p 68.

**R.M. Williams** CITY CENTER Authentic Australian country clothes. In the bush, you'll see the iconic elastic-sided boots, moleskin jeans, and Driza-Bone jackets everywhere. It's good gear that lasts forever.

*Dinosaur Designs.*

**Warning:** Wear anything other than the boots in Sydney and you'll look a bit silly. There are a number of outlets across the city but the one in The Rocks is pretty central. *71 George St.* ☎ 02/9247 0204. AE, DC, MC, V. Train: Circular Quay. Map p 68.

### Australian Designers

★★★ **Akira** CITY CENTER & WOOL-LAHRA With his smart tailoring and exquisite fabric, Japanese-born Akira Isogawa is one of Australia's most acclaimed designers. *Level 2, Strand Arcade.* ☎ 02/9232 1078. Train: Martin Place. 12a Queen St. ☎ 02/9361 5221. Bus: 389. AE, MC, V. Map p 67 and 68.

★★ **Alannah Hill** PADDINGTON Stilettos and boots, scarves and bags, dresses and jackets, and jewelry. If you like the romantic and whimsical, you'll love her stuff. *118–120 Oxford St.* ☎ 02/9380 9147. MC, V. Bus: 389. Map p 67.

★★★ **Alistair Trung** PADDING-TON & CITY CENTER Trung wants his clothes to challenge you. Best described as luxuriously slouchy, his intricately draped and sometimes voluminous clothes are designed to envelope and flatter real female bodies. *445 Oxford St. & QVB (see* above). ☎ 02/9331 5729 (Paddington) & 02/9267 8828 (QVB). MC, V. Bus 378, 380. Map p 67 and 68.

★★★ **Collette Dinnigan** WOOLLAHRA Delicately beaded, soft, silky, and floaty (and expensive) are the best ways to describe Dinnigan's famously feminine dresses. *104 Queen St.* ☎ *02/9363 2698. AE, MC, V. Bus: 380, 389, 378. Map p 67.*

★★ **Easton Pearson** PADDINGTON High-end women's fashion epitomizes bohemian luxe. Popular with those 35-plus. *18 Elizabeth St.* ☎ *02/9331 4433. AE, MC, V. Bus: 380, 389, 378. Map p 67.*

**Ksubi** BONDI Fans of Ksubi's (say Soo-bie) must-have jeans and silk T-shirts include Kate Moss, Madonna, Ashley Olsen, and Pete Doherty. *82 Gould St.* ☎ *02/9300 8233. MC, V. Bus: 380. Map p 67.*

★★★ **Lisa Ho** WOOLLAHRA Rich and glamorous high-end fashion that can actually be affordable even on a guidebook writer's wage (during sale time). *43 Queen St.* ☎ *02/9327 6300. AE, MC, V. Bus: 389. Map p 67.*

**Mr. Rose** PADDINGTON Beautifully tailored shirts for women and handmade accessories, including fabulous fabric flowers. *31 Norfolk St.* ☎ *02/9368 1423. MC, V. Bus: 378, 380. Map p 67.*

**Sass & Bide** PADDINGTON Famous for their sleek and sexy jeans so low they had a 2-inch fly, Sass & Bide is a favorite with fashionistas. *132 Oxford St.* ☎ *02/9360 3900. AE, MC, V. Bus: 378, 380. Map p 67.*

## Beachwear
**Bikini Island** BONDI Hundreds of bikinis in every size. *38 Campbell Parade.* ☎ *02/9300 9446. MC, V. Bus: 380. Map p 67.*

*Not for city slickers: R.M. Williams.*

★★ **Billabong** CITY CENTER Whether you want to actually get them wet or just look like you hang out on the beach all day, Billabong's the coolest teenage surf/skateboard label around. *Shop T7, Sydney Arcade, Pitt Street Mall.* ☎ *02/9223 0362. AE, MC, V. Train: Martin Place. Map p 68.*

★★ **Mambo** MANLY Another cool shop for surfer guys and girls, the original designs feature irreverent graphic artwork, although the brand has been colonized somewhat in the past few years by dads trying to look as cool as their teenage sons. *80 The Corso.*

*Alistair Trung.*

Lisa Ho.

☎ 02/9977 9171. AE, MC, V. Ferry: Manly. Map p 68.

## Books

### ★★ Berkelouw Books PADDINGTON
It's not just the extensive range of new, rare, and secondhand books that make this a favorite with bookworms, but the late opening hours—until 11pm most nights, midnight on Friday and Saturday. *19 Oxford St.* ☎ *02/9360 3200. AE, MC, V. Bus: 880, 378. Map p 67.*

### ★★ Better Read Than Dead
NEWTOWN It's not the biggest bookstore around, but it scores stars for the name alone and the staff here actually know about the books they sell. *265 King St.* ☎ *02/9557 8700. AE, MC, V. Train: Newtown. Map p 70.*

### ★★★ Gleebooks GLEBE
The best bookshop in Sydney as far as I'm concerned. Not only do they stock a huge range, but they host regular author events and other literary functions. The original Gleebooks just up the road (191 Glebe Point Rd.) specializes in children's, antiquarian, and secondhand titles.

See p 63, **3**. AE, MC, V. Bus: 431, 433. Map p 70.

### ★★★ Gould's Book Arcade
NEWTOWN See p 64, **8**. Map p 70.

**Kinokuniya** CITY CENTER There's a huge range of titles in this Japanese-owned bookstore, including Japanese and Chinese texts, as well as an extensive collection of manga, graphic novels, art and design books, cookbooks, travel books, and children's literature. *Level 2, The Galleries Victoria, 500 George St.* ☎ *02/9262 7996. AE, DC, MC, V. Train: Town Hall. Map p 68.*

## Department Stores

### ★★ David Jones CITY CENTER
Australia's oldest department store has branches in most large suburban shopping centers, but the two flagship stores in the city are worth visiting just for the basement food hall alone, where you can find almost every gourmet goodie. In spring the ground floor is transformed with flower displays and the animated Christmas window displays are a hit with kids. *65 Market St. & 86 Castlereagh St.* ☎ *02/9266 5544. AE, DC, MC, V. Train: Town Hall or Martin Place. Map p 68.*

**Myer** CITY CENTER You'll also find Myer stores scattered throughout the suburbs. Myer stores have the same range of goods as David Jones, but are slightly less upmarket. *436 George St.* ☎ *02/9238 9111. AE, DC, MC, V. Train: Martin Place. Map p 68.*

## Factory Outlets
**Market City** HAYMARKET East meets West in this shopping center above Paddy's Markets in Chinatown, so expect lots of cheap Chinese imports and specialty stores, as well as some good streetwear.

More than 30 factory outlets of top fashion brands and great *yum cha* in the food hall. *Corner Hay & Thomas sts.* ☎ *02/9288 8900. www.market city.com.au. Monorail: Paddy's Markets. Train: Central. Map p 68.*

### Hats & Bags

★★ **Crumpler** NEWTOWN Street-smart bags for laptops, cameras, phones, and whatever else you need to carry. You can even get your own design custom-made in the store. *305 King St.* ☎ *02/9565 1611. AE, MC, V. Train: Newtown. Map p 70.*

★★★ **Leo Monk Handbags** NEWTOWN Hand-crafted, limited edition colorful Italian leather designer bags that are surprisingly affordable. *417 King St.* ☎ *02/9557 5728. AE, DC, MC, V. Train: Newtown. Map p 70.*

★ **Strand Hatters** CITY CENTER From top hats and fedoras to the iconic Aussie Akubra, the Strand Hatters has been covering men's heads for the past 30 years. *The Strand Arcade, 412 George St.* ☎ *02/9231 6884. AE, MC, V. Train: Martin Place. Map p 68.*

### Markets

★ **Balmain Market** BALMAIN Tiny and very local, it's mainly bric-a-brac and preloved clothes, with a sprinkling of art and homewares. Good food inside the hall. *St. Andrews Church, corner Darling St. & Curtis Rd. Sat 8:30am–4pm. Bus: 442. Map p 70.*

★★★ **Bondi Markets** BONDI Best for vintage and retro clothing and to snag a piece from a (future) top designer. Look for celebrities slinking around the stalls, hiding behind their sunglasses. *Bondi Beach Public School, Campbell Parade. Sun 10am–5pm. Bus: 380. Map p 67.*

★★★ kids **Glebe Markets** GLEBE See p 63, ④. *Map p 70.*

★★ **Kirribilli Art, Design & Vintage Markets** MILSONS POINT Lots of art, jewelry, fashion, and other unique pieces, you'll never know what you might find here. It's affiliated with a vintage market (antiques, collectibles, and clothing) in neighboring Bradfield Park. *Burton St. Tunnel. Second Sun of the month, 9am–3pm. Train: Milsons Point. Map p 68.*

*Strand Hatters.*

*Birdland Records.*

### ★★★ Paddington Markets

PADDINGTON   Launching pad for most of Australia's, and certainly Sydney's, most famous fashion designers and the place to find quality contemporary art, craft, and fashion, sold to you by the artists and craft makers themselves. Go early, as it gets very crowded by early afternoon. *Paddington Uniting Church, 395 Oxford St. Sat 10am–4pm. Bus: 378, 380. Map p 67.*

### Paddy's Markets HAYMARKET

*See p 57, ➊. Map p 68.*

### ★ The Rocks Markets THE ROCKS

*See p 53, ➏. Map p 68.*

## Music

### ★★★ Birdland Records CITY

CENTER   Jazz, jazz, and more jazz. *Level 4, Dymocks Building, 428 George St. ☎ 02/9231 1188. AE, MC, V. Train: Martin Place. Map p 68.*

### ★ Red Eye Records CITY CENTER

Sydney's largest independent music retailer has everything from punk to Gothic and avant-garde—and anything-in-between. *143 York St. ☎ 02/9267 7440. 370 Pitt St. ☎ 02/9262 9755. AE, MC, V. Train: Martin Place & Museum. Map p 68.*

## Pajamas

### ★★★ Peter Alexander CITY

CENTER   The best winter pajamas, period. Don't be fooled by the pink stores; there are ranges for men and kids, too. Numerous stores in Sydney, but easiest to find is the one on Pitt Street Mall. *Pitt Street Mall. ☎ 02/9232 4941. AE, MC, V. Train: Martin Place. Map p 68.*

## Vintage & Recycled Fashion

### ★★★ Coco Repose SURRY HILLS

Hand-picked vintage gowns and dresses, and brand-new ones made from vintage fabric. *Sydney Antiques Centre, 531 South Dowling St. No phone. MC, V. Train: Central. Map p 68.*

### ★ Di Nuovo PADDINGTON   Recy-

cled designer fashion from Australia and overseas at up to half the price you would pay for brand-new. Everything's sold on consignment and stock changes every 2 months. *92 William St. ☎ 02/9361 4221. AE, MC, V. Bus: 378, 380. Map p 67.*

### ★★ Grandma Takes a Trip

SURRY HILLS & BONDI   Huge range of clothing and accessories from the '50s through to the '80s, all imported from the U.K. The Bondi store has a great collection of retro swimwear. *263 Crown St. ☎ 02/9356 3322 (Surry Hills). 79 Gould St. ☎ 02/9130 6262 (Bondi). MC, V. Bus: 380. Map p 67 and 68.*

### ★ Pelle PADDINGTON   Mint condi-

tion secondhand European designer footwear and accessories. *90 William St. ☎ 02/9331 8100. MC, V. Bus: 378, 380. Map p 67. ●*

# 5 The Best of the **Great Outdoors**

# Parks & Gardens

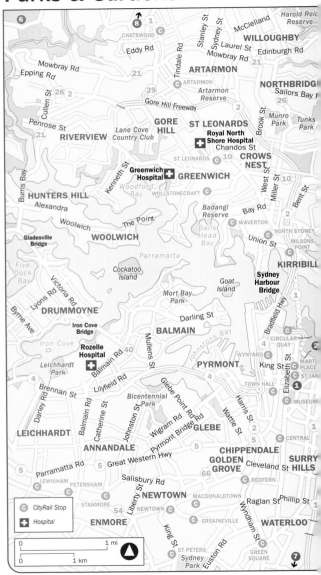

*Previous page: Bronte Baths.*

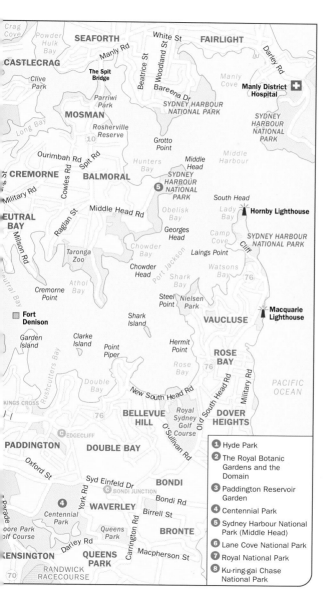

1 Hyde Park
2 The Royal Botanic Gardens and the Domain
3 Paddington Reservoir Garden
4 Centennial Park
5 Sydney Harbour National Park (Middle Head)
6 Lane Cove National Park
7 Royal National Park
8 Ku-ring-gai Chase National Park

Australia's largest city is also one of its greenest, and it's one of the few cities in the world that has national parks within easy reach. From the green oasis of the Royal Botanic Gardens and the expansive harbor views in Sydney Harbour National Park to the wild bushland of Ku-ring-gai, Sydney has plenty of places where you can escape the urban jungle and enjoy the great outdoors.

*Paddington Reservoir, designed and opened in 2008.*

① ★★ **Hyde Park.** Named after London's Hyde Park, this pocket of green that covers 2 large city blocks in the middle of the CBD was originally a racecourse. In the southern section you'll find the Art Deco War Memorial, built in 1934 as a tribute to those who died in WWI. In the northern section is the flamboyant Archibald Fountain—a bronze Apollo surrounded by horses' heads, dolphins, and tortoises—erected in 1932 to commemorate the ties between Australia and France in the same war. The two features are linked by an impressive fig-lined avenue. *Train: St. James or Museum.*

② ★★★ **The Royal Botanic Gardens and the Domain.** A favorite spot for a picnic or early morning walk, these gardens are home to more than a million specimens, some of which were planted by the First Fleeters 220 years ago. Don't miss the Sydney Tropical Centre in the glass pyramid and the Rare and Threatened Plants Garden, which includes the Wollemi Pine, thought to be extinct until recently. *Free 90-min. guided tours daily, 10:30am, plus 1pm Nov–Mar. Free admission, except Tropical Centre $5.50 adults, $3.30 kids, $11 for families. See also p 27,* ③*. Train: Martin Place.*

③ ★ **Paddington Reservoir Garden.** This sunken garden has been built at the bottom of an old water reservoir. It was decommissioned in 1899, became a storage facility and then a garage with a park on top—until the roof collapsed in 1990 when it became a graffiti grotto (the graffiti's still there, which adds to the delightfully shadowy atmosphere) and then was restored and reborn as a landscaped park, complete with an ornamental pond and hanging gardens around the edges. It feels very Romanesque and otherworldly. *Corner Oxford & Oatley sts., Paddington. Bus: 378, 380.*

④ ★★★ **kids Centennial Park.** This grand 189-hectare (467-acre) park was established in 1888 as part of the centenary celebrations and was also the site of the inauguration of the Australian Federation in 1901. The 10 ponds are popular picnic spots and the 3.6km (2¼-mile) Grand Drive is a favorite spot to walk, run, cycle, or rollerblade. It's one of the few inner city parks in the world where you can go horse riding. To book a horse ride or lesson (prices vary) contact the Centennial Parklands Equestrian Centre (☎ 02/9332 2809).

**5 ★★★ Sydney Harbour National Park.** Highlights, apart from the beautiful views, include convict-built buildings, and historic maritime and military installations. The best sections include ★ **Fort Denison** (p 23, **2**), the old ★★ **Q Station** on North Head (p 20, **9**), ★★★ **South Head** (p 32, **9**), ★★ **Nielsen Park** (p 33, **14**), and ★★ **Bradleys Head** near Taronga Zoo. The park includes the ★★★ **Manly Scenic Walkway,** a fantastic 9.5km (6-mile) walking trail that starts at the Spit and finishes at Manly—or vice versa. It hugs the shoreline almost the entire way. *Bus: 178 from Wynyard (Stand C). Ferry: Manly from Circular Quay.*

**6 ★ kids Lane Cove National Park.** The Lane Cove River winds through a peaceful bushland valley just beyond the backyard fences of lower north shore suburbia near Chatswood. It's one of the few places you can camp or park your caravan and still be within easy reach of the city center. There's also a luxury glamping option with

*Lane Cove.*

*Centennial Park.*

en-suite safari tents, see p 138. *Admission $7 per vehicle, per day, $4.40 otherwise. Bus: 545 from Chatswood Station.*

**7 ★★ Royal National Park.** The world's second-oldest national park (after Yellowstone in the U.S.) was established in 1879. Just 32km (20 miles) south of Sydney, the park features riverside picnic areas, surf beaches, cliff-top walks, and rainforest cycle tracks. *Sir Bertram Stevens Dr., Audley. Admission $11 per vehicle, per day. Camping fees $5–$14 adults, $3–$7 kids. Bookings essential. Train: Engadine or Heathcote.*

**8 ★★ kids Ku-ring-gai Chase National Park.** On the northern edge of Sydney's suburban sprawl, the Hawkesbury River meets the sea in this popular park. You can swim at sheltered beaches; follow walking trails through heathland and along sandstone ridges; and go boating, fishing, canoeing, or mountain biking. Camp at the Basin ($14 adults, $7 kids), but bookings are essential. *See p 45, **9**. ☎ 02/9974 1011. Admission $11 per vehicle, per day. Train: Berowra. Bus: 190 from Wynyard to Palm Beach. Ferry: Palm Beach Wharf to the Basin.*

# Sporty Sydney

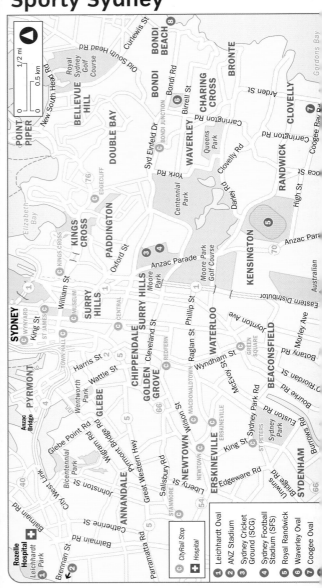

N

0    1/2 mi
0    0.5 km

**SYDNEY**

POINT PIPER

BELLEVUE HILL

Royal Sydney Golf Course

New South Head Rd

Old South Head Rd

Curlewis St

BONDI BEACH ❽

BONDI

Bondi Rd

BRONTE

Arden St

CHARING CROSS

Carrington Rd

Birrell St

WAVERLEY ❻

Queens Park

Clovelly Rd

CLOVELLY ❼

Carrington Rd

Coogee Bay Rd

RANDWICK

High St

Anzac Para

Gordons Bay

DOUBLE BAY

BONDI JUNCTION

Syd Einfeld Dr

York Rd

Centennial Park

Daley Rd

KENSINGTON ❺

Australian

EDGECLIFF

Elizabeth Bay

KINGS CROSS

PADDINGTON

Oxford St

❸ ❹

Anzac Parade

Moore Park

Moore Park Golf Course

Eastern Distributor

William St

King St

Wynyard

St James

Museum

Central

Surry Hills

SURRY HILLS

CHIPPENDALE

Cleveland St

GOLDEN GROVE

Harris St

Wattle St

Wentworth Park

Wilson St

Raglan St

Phillip St

WATERLOO

Wyndham St

McEvoy St

GREEN SQUARE

Joynton Ave

Redfern

BEACONSFIELD

Botany Rd

Morley Ave

O'Riordan St

Bourke Rd

PYRMONT

Anzac Bridge

Glebe Point Rd

GLEBE

Wigram Rd

Bicentennial Park

Pyrmont Bridge Rd

Great Western Hwy

Salisbury Rd

ANNANDALE

Johnston St

Catherine St

City West Link

Balmain Rd

Balmain Rd

Brennan St

Rozelle Hospital

Leichhardt ❶

Leichhardt Park

Parramatta Rd

STANMORE

NEWTOWN

MACDONALDTOWN

King St

Liberty St

Edgeware Rd

ERSKINEVILLE

ST PETERS

Sydney Park Rd

Sydney Park

Euston Rd

Burrows Rd

Unwins Bridge Rd

SYDENHAM

Bridge Rd

---

❷ CityRail Stop

✚ Hospital

① Leichhardt Oval
② ANZ Stadium
③ Sydney Cricket Ground (SCG)
④ Sydney Football Stadium (SFS)
⑤ Royal Randwick
⑥ Waverley Oval
⑦ Coogee Oval

**S**ydneysiders love their sport. In summer it's cricket, in winter it's footy—which in Sydney means rugby league, not soccer—or Aussie Rules (AFL), which is what they play in Victoria (and just about everywhere else but Queensland). Catch the sporting fever!

*Sydney Cricket Ground.*

**❶ Sydney Cricket Ground (SCG).** Home to the best of Sydney's cricket since 1810, the SCG usually hosts one test match each year (in Dec or Jan), several 1-day internationals (in Dec–Jan), as well as a number of 20/20 games. The cheapest first-class games are usually those between state teams in the Sheffield Shield series (the name

## Cricket

A cricket fan is called a cricket tragic, and Australia's national game is followed by everyone from the former prime minister John Howard (a self-confessed cricket tragic) on down. After all, what's not to love about a game that takes 5 days to play (and even then often ends in a draw) and breaks for afternoon tea? Traditionalists will tell you the only match worth following is the international test series, where each team plays up to five 5-day matches to decide the winner, but it's the Ashes series between Australia and England that really ignites passions. Played in alternate countries every 4 years, the series dates back to 1882 and the trophy is a small urn containing the ashes of a cricket ball. The 1-day series and 2½-hour-long 20/20 series are fast-paced and generally more exciting, although they are derided by *true* cricket tragics as "pajama cricket" in reference to the colorful uniforms worn by players.

# Rugby League

Watching the crowd roar at a footy game is to see Sydney at its most tribal. The main competition is in the National Rugby League (NRL), which has 16 teams and culminates in the Grand Final in late September/early October. It draws a big crowd—up to 80,000—and has the majority of Sydneysiders glued to their TVs. The city also stops for the three evening State of Origin games between New South Wales (NSW, the Blues or the Cockroaches) and Queensland (QLD, the Maroons or Cane Toads) in May/June.

changes with the sponsors). The SCG is also home ground to the Sydney Swans, Sydney's only team in the AFL (Aussie Rules) competition. *Driver Ave., Moore Park.* ☎ *02/9360 6601. www.scgt.nsw.gov.au for match details. www.ticketek.com.au for tickets. Ticket prices vary. Bus: 339, 373, 374, 392, 394.*

**②** **Waverley Oval.** On any summer weekend you'll find cricket ovals all around the city and suburbs resounding to the crack of willow as another ball is hit for six (over the fence) in the Sydney Grade competition. You can usually watch these matches for free. *Bondi Rd. Bus: 380.*

**③** **Royal Randwick.** The sport of kings is alive and well in Sydney with four major racecourses at Rosehill, Warwick Farm, Canterbury, and Randwick. Despite it being an outdoor event, you are expected to dress up for the carnival races—women wear their fanciest hats. *Alison Rd. www.ajc.org.au for race dates. Admission prices vary. Bus: 372, 373, 374, 377.*

**④** **ANZ Stadium.** The former Olympic Games venue is home ground to five NRL teams, so there's a game most Saturdays and Sundays during the season. Except for grand finals and State of Origin games, it seldom fills to capacity,

*Horse racing in Sydney.*

*Waratahs rugby match.*

which can make games seem a little soulless. *Sydney Olympic Park.* ☎ *132 849. www.anzstadium.com. au. www.ticketek.com.au for tickets. Ticket prices vary. Train: Olympic Park.*

**5 Sydney Football Stadium (SFS).** Home ground of eastern suburbs NRL team the Sydney Roosters as well as A-league soccer team the Sydney FC. *Next door to the Sydney Cricket Ground (see 1, above).*

**6 Leichhardt Oval.** A great place to get close to the action. It only holds three NRL games a year so tickets can be hard to get, but there is usually some sort of footy played here each Saturday. *Glover St.* ☎ *02/9556 0400. Ticket prices vary. Bus: 440.*

**7 Coogee Oval.** Always atmospheric is a Galloping Greens game at the home ground of Sydney's most famous rugby league club, Randwick. *Brook St. www.randwick rugby.com.au. $15 adults, kids free. Sat 3pm, late March to end Sept. Bus: 372, 373, 374.*

**8 Surf Carnivals.** Being a surf lifesaver is about much more than patrolling the beach and saving damsels (and dudes) in distress. "Surf sports" covers beach- and rescue-oriented events, including combined swimming and running, surf skiing, and surf boating races for all ages, including nippers as young as 5. Dates and locations of surf carnivals can be found at www.surflifesaving. com.au.

*A colorful Surf Carnival.*

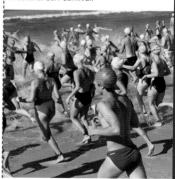

# Rugby Union

Rugby union is not as popular as rugby league. The New South Wales team, the Waratahs, play at the Sydney Football Stadium (SFS, see 5, above), but the game to catch is the Bledisloe Cup between Australia's Wallabies and New Zealand's All Blacks, where trans-Tasman rivalries run high. If it's in Australia it's played at the ANZ Stadium (see 4, above). See www.rugby.com.au for details.

# Ocean & Harbor Pools

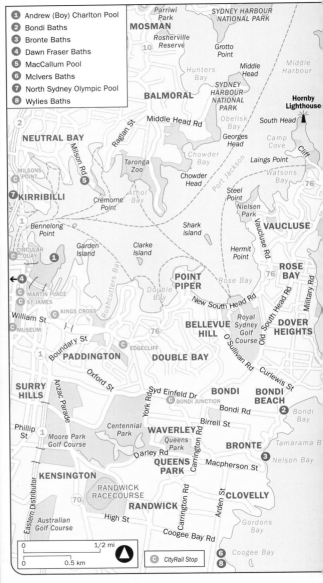

1. Andrew (Boy) Charlton Pool
2. Bondi Baths
3. Bronte Baths
4. Dawn Fraser Baths
5. MacCallum Pool
6. McIvers Baths
7. North Sydney Olympic Pool
8. Wylies Baths

SYDNEY HARBOUR NATIONAL PARK
Parriwi Park
MOSMAN
Rosherville Reserve
Grotto Point
Hunters Bay
Middle Head
Middle Harbour
SYDNEY HARBOUR NATIONAL PARK
Hornby Lighthouse
South Head
BALMORAL
Obelisk Bay
Middle Head Rd
Georges Head
Camp Cove
Raglan St
Taronga Zoo
Chowder Bay
Laings Point
Cliff
NEUTRAL BAY
Milson Rd
Chowder Head
Port Jackson
Watsons Bay
76
MILSONS POINT
Athol Bay
Steel Point
KIRRIBILLI
Cremorne Point
Nielsen Park
VAUCLUSE
Bennelong Point
Shark Island
Hermit Point
Vaucluse Rd
CIRCULAR QUAY
Garden Island
Clarke Island
ROSE BAY
MARTIN PLACE
ST JAMES
Double Bay
POINT PIPER
Rose Bay
76
DOVER HEIGHTS
William St
KINGS CROSS
Rushcutters Bay
New South Head Rd
South Head Rd
Old
Military Rd
MUSEUM
BELLEVUE HILL
Royal Sydney Golf Course
O'Sullivan Rd
Boundary St
EDGECLIFF
76
Curlewis St
PADDINGTON
DOUBLE BAY
Oxford St
SURRY HILLS
Anzac Parade
Syd Einfeld Dr
BONDI JUNCTION
BONDI
BONDI BEACH
York Rd
Bondi Rd
2
Bondi Bay
Phillip St
Centennial Park
Birrell St
Moore Park Golf Course
WAVERLEY
Queens Park
BRONTE
Tamarama B
Darley Rd
Carrington Rd
Macpherson St
3
Nelson Bay
QUEENS PARK
KENSINGTON
RANDWICK RACECOURSE
Carrington Rd
Arden St
CLOVELLY
70
RANDWICK
High St
Gordons Bay
Eastern Distributor
Australian Golf Course
Coogee Bay Rd
6
8
Coogee Bay

0 — 1/2 mi
0 — 0.5 km

C CityRail Stop

Egalitarian to their core, Sydney's plunge-worthy ocean and harbor pools are favorites of Olympic champions and playful paddlers alike. Whether they are washed over by rolling ocean waves or calmly perched on the harbor's edge, with views this good you'll soon be swapping your Australian crawl for a breast-stroke or backstroke. Who wants to stare at the bottom of the pool when you could be lapping up harbor or beach views?

**1 Andrew (Boy) Charlton Pool.** In the heart of the Botanic Gardens with views across the Woolloomooloo side of the harbor, this is one of the few outdoor pools that are heated. Named after the 1920s Australian swimming legend, it is believed to be the birthplace of the Australian crawl (freestyle) swimming stroke. Not surprisingly, laps are the order of the day and it's popular with the before- and after-work crowd. *Mrs. Macquaries Rd.* ☎ *02/9358 6686. www.abcpool.org. Admission $5.80 adults, $4.40 kids. Daily 6am–7pm (8pm daylight saving). Train: Martin Place and walk to the Royal Botanic Gardens.*

**2 ★★ Bondi Baths.** More commonly known as Bondi Icebergs. *See p 14,* **4**.

**3 ★★★ Bronte Baths.** Built into the rock at the southern end of Bronte Beach in 1887 by the local council to cater to the new "sea-bathing fad," it was originally men-only on Sundays and public holidays. While the rules and fashions may have changed, the original irregularly shaped structure remains largely intact. It can be a little challenging in choppy seas. *Bronte Rd. Free admission. Daily, unless closed for cleaning (usually at low tide) or because of rough weather. Bus: 378.*

*Bronte Beach bathers.*

**④ ★★★ kids Dawn Fraser Baths.** The oldest pool and swimming club in Australia, the Victorian-era Elkington Park Baths were renamed in honor of the gold medal champion, a Balmain girl who learned to swim and trained here (Dawn still lives in Balmain). At low tide there is a small sandy beach that is great for kids. *Fitzroy Ave.* ☎ *02/9555 1903. Admission $4.20 adults, $3 kids. Daily 7:15am–6:30pm (6:45am–7pm daylight saving) from Oct long weekend (usually 1st weekend in Oct) to Easter Monday. Bus: 433.*

**⑤ ★★★ MacCallum Pool.** Every single one of these harborside and ocean pools has a great view, but if I had to pick the best, I'd name this 1920s lap pool. It's long and only two lanes wide, but it has knockout views of the Opera House, Harbour Bridge, and city skyline. No wonder the sidestroke's so popular here! The timber deck is the place to soak up the sun. *Milson Rd. Free admission. Daily (closed for cleaning for approximately 6 hr., usually on a Thurs or Fri). Ferry: Cremorne Point.*

*North Sydney Olympic Pool.*

**⑥ ★★★ kids McIvers Baths.** Also known as Ladies' or Women's Baths, this 20m (66-ft.) ocean pool perched on a cliff face is reserved for women and children only—and has been since 1876. It is the last remaining women-only seawater pool in Australia and has an exemption under the New South Wales Anti-Discrimination Act. The track to the pool is steep, but the pool is well screened so it's great for anyone who likes their privacy. *Grant Reserve, Beach St. Free admission. Daily. Bus: 372, 373, 374.*

**⑦ ★★ North Sydney Olympic Pool.** I always get distracted by the grinning face of Luna Park and the massive overhead arches of the Harbour Bridge, but that hasn't stopped better swimmers than me from setting 86 world records at this pool. It's heated and also offers regular yoga and Pilates classes. *4 Alfred St. South.* ☎ *02/9955 2309. Admission $6.70 adults, $3.30 kids. Mon–Fri 5:30am–9pm; Sat–Sun 7am–7pm. Train: Milsons Point.*

**⑧ ★★★ Wylies Baths.** Another historic rock pool, this one was built in 1907 by Henry Alexander Wylie, a champion long-distance and underwater swimmer whose daughter Wilhelmina won a silver medal in the 1912 Olympics—the first time women were allowed to compete in the swimming events. (Her best friend, Fanny Durack, won gold.) *Neptune St.* ☎ *02/9665 2838. www. wylies.com.au. Admission $4.50 adults, $1.50 kids. Daily 7am–5pm (7pm daylight saving). Bus: 372, 373, 374.*

### Tip

Swimming goggles are a must-have accessory at these pools, as saltwater can sting your eyes, and even the cleanest seawater can be murky sometimes. ●

# 6 The Best **Dining**

# Dining **Best Bets**

Best for Breakfast
★★★ Bills $ 359 Crown St. (p 96)

Best for Brunch
★★ Swell $ 465 Bronte Rd. (p 103)

Best by the Sea
★★★ The Bathers' Pavilion $$$$
4 The Esplanade (p 96)

Best BYO
★★ Ripples $$ North Sydney Olym-
pic Pool, Olympic Dr. (p 102)

Best Chinese
★★★ Billy Kwong $$$ Shop 3,
355 Crown St. (p 96)

Most French
★★ Claude's $$$$$ 10 Oxford St.
(p 98)

Best Harbor Views
★★★ Quay $$$$$ Overseas Pas-
senger Terminal (p 102)

Best Hotel Dining Room
★★ Glass $$$$ Hilton Hotel, 488
George St. (p 99)

Best Italian
★★★ Fratelli Paradiso $$
12–16 Challis Ave. (p 99)

Best Long Lunch
★★★ Catalina $$$$ Lyne Park (next
to Rose Bay Wharf) (p 98)

Most Romantic
★★★ ARIA $$$$$ 1 Macquarie St.
(p 96)

Best Seafood
★★★ The Boathouse on Blackwat-
tle Bay $$$$ End of Ferry Rd.
(p 97)

Best Southeast Asian
★★★ Longrain $$$ 85 Common-
wealth St. (p 100)

Best Splurge
★★★ Tetsuyas $$$$$ 529 Kent St.
(p 104)

Best Value
Spice I Am $ 90 Wentworth St.
(p 103)

Best Yum Cha
★★ Marigold Citymark $$ Levels
4 & 5, 683 George St. (p 101)

## BYO

Many smaller restaurants and neighborhood eateries in Sydney
are BYO (bring your own) which means you can bring a bottle of
wine—or beer—with you, even if they are licensed, although some
may charge a corkage fee of a few dollars. Either way, it's a great
way to save money.

*Previous page: Flying Fish restaurant.*

# Eastern Suburbs Dining

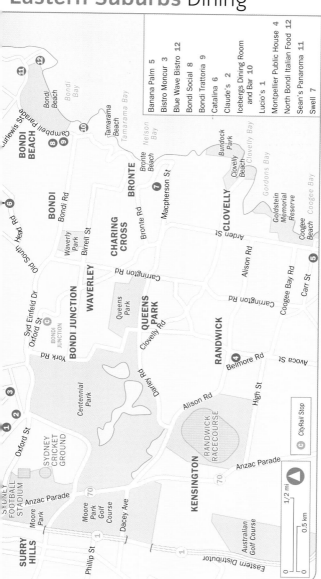

Banana Palm 5
Bistro Moncur 3
Blue Wave Bistro 12
Bondi Social 8
Bondi Trattoria 9
Catalina 6
Claude's 2
Icebergs Dining Room and Bar 10
Lucio's 1
Montpellier Public House 4
North Bondi Italian Food 12
Sean's Panaroma 11
Swell 7

# Inner Sydney Dining

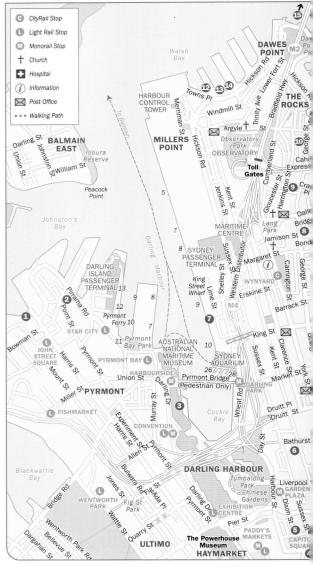

**Legend:**

- C CityRail Stop
- L Light Rail Stop
- M Monorail Stop
- † Church
- ✚ Hospital
- (i) Information
- ✉ Post Office
- --- Walking Path

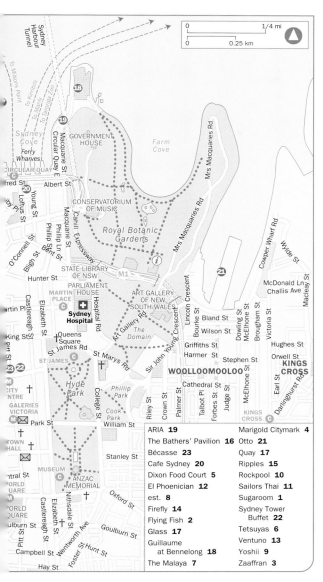

ARIA **19**

The Bathers' Pavilion **16**

Bécasse **23**

Cafe Sydney **20**

Dixon Food Court **5**

El Phoenician **12**

est. **8**

Firefly **14**

Flying Fish **2**

Glass **17**

Guillaume
    at Bennelong **18**

The Malaya **7**

Marigold Citymark **4**

Otto **21**

Quay **17**

Ripples **15**

Rockpool **10**

Sailors Thai **11**

Sugaroom **1**

Sydney Tower
    Buffet **22**

Tetsuyas **6**

Ventuno **13**

Yoshii **9**

Zaaffran **3**

# Kings Cross Dining

POTTS POINT

| | 1/8 mi |
| 0 | 0.125 km |

**C** CityRail Stop

**+** Hospital

St Neot Ave
Wylde St
McDonald Ln
Challis Ave **4**

Cowper Wharf Rd
Billyard Ave
Ithaca Rd

Bland St
Nicholson St
Wilson St
Plunkett St

Dowling St
McElhone St
Brougham St
Victoria St

Maclay St
Onslow Ave
Greenknowe Ave

ELIZABETH BAY

Harmer St
Stephen St

WOOLLOOMOOLOO

Hughes St **2**
Orwell St

KINGS CROSS **5**

Roslyn Gardens
Rushcutte Bay Park
Waratah St

Cathedral St
McElhone St

Earl St **3**
Darlinghurst Rd

Ward Ave
Roslyn St

**+** St Luke's Hospital

Talbot Pl
Forbes St
Judge St

KINGS CROSS

**C** KINGS CROSS

Bayswater Rd
Clement St
Bayswater

William St
Kings Cross Rd
entrance to
Cross City Tunnel
Craigend St

Forbes St
Clapton Pl

Kirketon Rd
Darlinghurst Rd
Victoria St
Nimrod St
Surrey St
Womerah Ave
Barcom Ave
McLachlan Ave

DARLINGHURST

Thomson St

Liverpool St **1**

West St

Boundary St
Nelld Ave

Burton St
Green Park
Glenview Ln
Glenview St
Brown St
Stephen St

Forbes St

Barcom Ave
**+** St Vincent's Private Hospital
Macdonald St
Liverpool St

Sturt St
Taylor St

Victoria St
West St
Boundary St
Comber St
Campbell Ave
Hopewell St

Fish Face **1**
Fratelli Paradiso **4**
jimmy liks **3**
Macleay Street Bistro
Mezzaluna **2**

# Surry Hills Dining

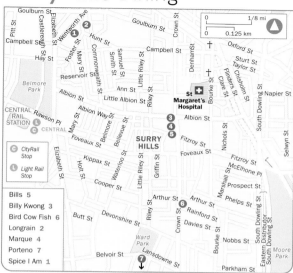

Bills 5
Billy Kwong 3
Bird Cow Fish 6
Longrain 2
Marque 4
Porteno 7
Spice I Am 1

# Glebe Dining

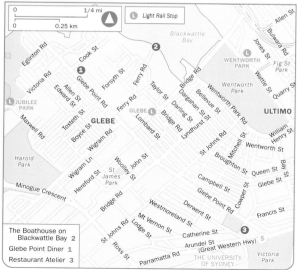

The Boathouse on
Blackwattle Bay 2
Glebe Point Diner 1
Restaurant Atelier 3

# Sydney **Restaurants A to Z**

★★★ **ARIA** EAST CIRCULAR QUAY
*CONTEMPORARY* Fine dining with
killer views of the Opera House and
harbor. Food is high-class and high
cost so dress to impress. *1 Macquarie St.* ☎ *02/9252 2555. www.
ariarestaurant.com. Mains $46–$58.
AE, DC, MC, V. Lunch Mon–Fri, dinner
daily. Train: Circular Quay. Map
p 92.*

**Banana Palm** COOGEE *VIETNAMESE* Very Indo-French and elegant
with lots of dark wood paneling and
historic black-and-white photos of a
vanished Vietnam. The only downside is there's no pho. *260 Arden St.,
Coogee.* ☎ *02/9665 1212. Mains
$19–$23. AE, DC, MC, V. Dinner Mon–
Sat. Bus: 372, 373, 374. Map p 91.*

★★★ **The Bathers' Pavilion** BALMORAL BEACH *CONTEMPORARY/
FRENCH* The perfect place for a
long, long lunch, this airy restaurant
on beautiful Balmoral Beach serves
seasonal produce with French flair.
*4 The Esplanade.* ☎ *02/9969 5050.
www.batherspavilion.com.au. Mains
$48. AE, DC, MC, V. Breakfast Sun,
lunch & dinner daily. Bus: 247 from
Wynyard. Map p 92.*

★★ **Bécasse** CITY CENTER *FRENCH*
Don't be put off that Bécasse is in a
shopping mall; it's among Sydney's
most highly awarded fine dining. A
good choice if you're eager to
impress. Dinner is degustation
menu only. *Level 5, Westfield Sydney, corner of Pitt Street Mall and
Market sts.* ☎ *02/9283 3440. www.
becasse.com.au. Lunch, 3 courses
$120; 7-course degustation $170.
AE, DC, MC, V. Lunch & dinner Mon–
Sat. Train: Martin Place. Map p 92.*

★★★ **kids** **Bills** SURRY HILLS *CONTEMPORARY* This bright and vibey
cafe is legendary for delicious
breakfasts of divine scrambled eggs
and ricotta hot cakes. The lunch and
dinner menus prove that you don't
have to spend a fortune to eat well.
There are also Bills restaurants in
Darlinghurst and Woollahra. *359
Crown St.* ☎ *02/9360 4762. www.
bills.com.au. Breakfast $6–$25,
mains $21–$31. AE, MC, V. Breakfast, lunch, & dinner daily. Bus: 378,
380. Map p 95.*

★★★ **Billy Kwong** SURRY HILLS
*CHINESE* The seats are uncomfortable, you have to queue to get in

*Fresh fish at The Boathouse on Blackwattle Bay.*

*Tempura zucchini blossoms with goat ricotta, at Cafe Sydney.*

because they won't take bookings, and the room is tiny, but celebrity TV chef Kylie Kwong uses organic, biodynamic, fair-trade, and ethically farmed produce to create some of the best Chinese food in the city. *Shop 3, 355 Crown St.* ☎ *02/9332 3300. www.kyliekwong.org. Mains $22–$48. AE, MC, V. Dinner Mon–Sat. Bus: 378, 380. Map p 95.*

★★ **Bistro Moncur** WOOLLAHRA *FRENCH* This fabulous Parisian-style bistro is nestled in the back room of the Woollahra Hotel. The Sirloin Café de Paris is hard to beat. *116 Queen St.* ☎ *02/9327 9713. www.woollahra hotel.com.au. Mains $30–$44. AE, DC, MC, V. Lunch Tues–Sun, dinner daily. Bus: 389. Map p 91.*

**Blue Wave Bistro** BONDI *CON-TEMPORARY* You get the same view as at the much more fashionable North Bondi Italian Food downstairs (p 101), but the food's half the price. Okay, so the food's not quite as classy (nor are the diners), but with deals like $8 steaks on Wednesdays, who's complaining? There is a catch; it's an RSL club (Returned Services League) so only those that don't live locally can sign in as guests; if you live within 5km (3 miles) you'll have to join ($20 annually). *North Bondi RSL, 120 Ramsgate*

*Ave., North Bondi.* ☎ *02/9130 3152. Mains $12–$25. Lunch & dinner daily. Bus: 380, 389. Map p 91.*

★★★ **The Boathouse on Blackwattle Bay** GLEBE *SEAFOOD* Famous for its wide selection of oysters and an amazing snapper pie, the Boathouse knows how to cook fish. *End of Ferry Rd.* ☎ *02/9518 9011. www.boathouse.net.au. Mains $36–$48. AE, DC, MC, V. Lunch & dinner Tues–Sun (open Mon in Dec). Bus: 434, 431. Map p 95.*

★★★ **Bondi Social** BONDI *CON-TEMPORARY* Tapas-size tasting plates make this a great place to get together with friends on the balcony overlooking Bondi Beach. *Level 1, 38 Campbell Parade.* ☎ *02/9365 1788. www.bondisocial.com. Mains $16–$20. MC, V. Lunch Sat–Sun, dinner daily. Bus: 380. Map p 91.*

★★ **Bondi Trattoria** BONDI *ITAL-IAN* A favorite neighborhood eatery with great food, friendly service, and fabulous beach views. The outside tables are a top spot to soak up the winter sun. *34 Campbell Parade.* ☎ *02/9365 4303. www.bondi trattoria.com.au. Mains $27–$34. AE, MC, V. Breakfast, lunch, & dinner daily. Bus: 380. Map p 91.*

*An artful dish at Catalina.*

### ★★ Cafe Sydney CIRCULAR QUAY
*CONTEMPORARY/SEAFOOD*
Don't be fooled by the name, this stylish restaurant on the fifth floor of the historic Customs House at the Quay overlooking Harbour Bridge does not serve your standard cafe fare. Popular among business types at lunch, but a more eclectic crowd in the evenings. *31 Alfred St.* ☎ *02/ 9251 8683. www.cafesydney.com. Mains $34–$39. AE, DC, MC, V. Lunch Sun–Fri, dinner Mon–Sat. Train: Circular Quay. Map p 92.*

*Lebanese treats at El-Phoenician.*

### ★★★ Catalina ROSE BAY *CON-TEMPORARY* It's difficult to drag your eyes away from the expansive harbor view, but you'll find the food a worthy distraction—particularly the sushi. Swish, stylish, and special, especially at sunset. *Lyne Park (next to Rose Bay Wharf).* ☎ *02/9371 0555. www.catalinarosebay.com.au. Mains $42–$48. AE, DC, MC, V. Lunch daily, dinner Mon–Sat. Ferry: Rose Bay. Bus: 325, 323. Map p 91.*

### ★★ Claude's WOOLLAHRA
*FRENCH* Old school and old style. From the outside you'd hardly know this unassuming terrace is home to one of Sydney's top French restaurants. *10 Oxford St.* ☎ *02/9331 2325. www.claudes.com.au. Mains $38–$40. 5-course tasting menu $110, 8 courses $135. AE, DC, MC, V. Dinner Tues–Sat. Bus: 389. Map p 91.*

### ★ El-Phoenician WALSH BAY *LEB-ANESE* Suburban Sydney has some great Lebanese restaurants but they tend to be either downmarket affairs or upscale kebab shops. This restaurant is all class. Belly dancers on Friday and Saturday nights add a touch of fun. *7 Towns Place.* ☎ *02/9633 1611. www.el-phoenician.com.au. Mains $25–$38. AE, DC, MC, V. Lunch & dinner Tues–Sun. Train: Circular Quay. Map p 92.*

**est.** CITY CENTER *CONTEMPORARY*
This elegant restaurant in the Establishment Hotel is the perfect place to entertain if you're on a business expense account. *252 George St. ☎ 02/9240 3010. www.merivale. com. Mains $39–$59. AE, DC, MC, V. Lunch Mon–Fri, dinner Mon–Sat. Train: Wynyard. Map p 92.*

★★ **Firefly** WALSH BAY *TAPAS*
This breezy tapas bar with water views is a great place for a pre- or postshow nibble if you are heading to the Wharf Theatre. I love the duck and shallot pancakes and the prosciutto-wrapped haloumi. The eight-course banquet is a good value at $44. *Pier Seven, 17 Hickson Rd. ☎ 02/9241 2031. www.fireflybar. com.au. Mains $14–$19. AE, MC, V. Lunch & dinner Mon–Sat. Train: Circular Quay. Map p 92.*

**Fish Face** DARLINGHURST *SEAFOOD* Absolutely outstanding fish and chips, but the service can be patchy and seating can be cramped. If you can't get a table, opt for takeaway. *132 Darlinghurst Rd. ☎ 02/9332 4803. Mains $33–$40. AE, MC, V. Dinner daily. Train: Kings Cross. Map p 94.*

**Flying Fish** PYRMONT *SEAFOOD* Fine fish in a stunningly renovated wharf warehouse with great views of the working harbor. *19 Pirrama Rd. (Jones Bay Wharf). ☎ 02/9518 6677. www.flyingfish.com.au. Mains $41–$49. AE, DC, MC, V. Lunch Tues– Fri & Sun, dinner Mon–Sat. Water taxi or bus: 443, 449. Map p 92.*

★★★ **Fratelli Paradiso** POTTS POINT *ITALIAN* Great value Italian trattoria with an ever-changing blackboard menu. They don't take bookings so get there early. *12 Challis Ave. ☎ 02/9357 1744. www. fratelliparadiso.com. Mains $29–$35. AE, DC, MC, V. Breakfast & lunch daily, dinner Mon–Sat. Train: Kings Cross. Map p 94.*

*Cooking with fresh produce at Glass.*

★★ **Glass** CITY CENTER *CONTEMPORARY/FRENCH* Mix New York style with fresh Sydney produce and French flavors and you get Glass, where the food tastes as good as the room looks. There's usually someone rich and famous at a nearby table. *Hilton Hotel, 488 George St. ☎ 02/ 9265 6068. www.glassbrasserie.com. au. Mains $42–$68. AE, DC, MC, V. Lunch Mon–Fri, dinner daily. Train: Town Hall. Map p 97.*

**kids Glebe Point Diner** GLEBE *CONTEMPORARY* Good hearty food that will have you coming back to this popular local eatery for more, even though the service can be rushed at times. *407 Glebe Point Rd. ☎ 02/9660 2646. www.glebe pointdiner.com.au. Mains $28–$36. MC, V. Lunch Fri–Sun, dinner Mon– Sat. Bus: 434, 431. Map p 95.*

★★★ **Guillaume at Bennelong** CIRCULAR QUAY *CONTEMPORARY/ FRENCH* You would expect a restaurant in a tourist icon like the Opera House to be a rip-off, but Guillaume at Bennelong is anything but. Sure, it's pricey, but it's worth it if you're planning a special night out. The three-course pretheater menu is an excellent value, even if you are not going to a show afterward.

Catch is you'll have to eat at 5:30pm—but at least you get to watch the sun set behind the Harbour Bridge. *Sydney Opera House, Bennelong Point.* ☎ *02/9241 1999. www.guillaumeatbennelong.com.au. Mains $43–$60. Pretheater menu 2 courses $66, 3 courses $78. AE, DC, MC, V. Lunch Thurs–Fri, dinner Tues–Sat. Train: Circular Quay. Map p 92.*

### Icebergs Dining Room and Bar BONDI MEDITERRANEAN

Mix with Sydney's beautiful and glamorous at this drop-dead gorgeous clifftop bar and restaurant overlooking the iconic Bondi Icebergs swimming pool, and, of course, that beach. *1 Notts Ave.* ☎ *02/9365 9000. www.idrb.com. Mains $23–$46. AE, DC, MC, V. Lunch & dinner Tues–Sun. Bus: 380. Map p 91.*

### ★★★ jimmy liks POTTS POINT SOUTHEAST ASIAN

It's very hip and groovy, but don't let that put you off joining the long shared table—the food here is fantastic. Try "jimmy's selection," a great value eight-course banquet that showcases the best of the menu. *186 Victoria St.* ☎ *02/8354 1400. www.jimmyliks.com/restaurant.html. Mains $22–$35. 8-course selection $58. AE, MC, V. Dinner daily. Train: Kings Cross. Map p 94.*

### ★★★ Longrain SURRY HILLS THAI

Sophisticated cocktails match the food at Longrain. Just as well—the no-bookings policy means you'll probably spend some time at the bar before joining the communal table. But believe me, it's worth the wait for the egg net (stuffed with pork, prawns, peanuts, and bean sprouts) alone. *85 Commonwealth St.* ☎ *02/9280 2888. www.longrain.com.au. Mains $28–$42. AE, DC, MC, V. Lunch Mon–Fri, dinner daily. Train: Central or Museum. Map p 95.*

### ★★★ Lucio's PADDINGTON ITALIAN

The amazing Australian art collection that decorates the walls of this restaurant is almost reason enough to come, but the seasonal Italian food is simply superb. Pricey, but worth it. *47 Windsor St.* ☎ *02/9380 5996. www.lucios.com.au. Mains $40–$45. AE, DC, MC, V. Lunch & dinner Mon–Sat. Bus: 378, 380. Map p 91.*

### Macleay Street Bistro POTTS POINT CONTEMPORARY

Great little local BYO eatery with no-fuss food that means it's always busy, so best to book. *73a Macleay St.* ☎ *02/9358 4891. Mains $28–$35. MC, V. Dinner daily. Train: Kings Cross. Map p 94.*

*Diners enjoy Italian classics at Mezzaluna.*

# King of the (Food) Court

For a wide choice of good, cheap, Asian food, you can't do much better than **Dixon House Food Court,** at the corner of Dixon and Little Hay streets in Haymarket (map p 92). It's home to around 14 or 15 food outlets, offering everything from *nasi lemak* and *roti chanai,* to beef pho, freshly squeezed sugar cane juice, and steamed pork buns, with cuisines stretching all the way from China and Nepal to Japan, Korea, Vietnam, Malaysia, and Indonesia—and almost all of it will see you get change from a $10 note. It's open daily 10:30am to 8:30pm.

★ **The Malaya** KING STREET WHARF *MALAYSIAN* Famous for their *laksa,* but the beef *rendang* is also pretty good. *39 Lime St.* ☎ *02/9279 1170. www.themalaya. com.au. Mains $24–$35. AE, DC, MC, V. Lunch Mon–Sat, dinner daily. Train: Wynyard. Map p 92.*

★★ kids **Marigold Citymark** HAYMARKET *CHINESE* In the heart of Chinatown, the Marigold is one of Sydney's best spots for weekend *yum cha* (small plates) The 800 seats fill fast, but the service is faster. I love the $25 dim sum degustation menu (Sun–Thurs dinner only). *Levels 4 & 5, 683–689 George St.* ☎ *02/9281 3388. www. marigold.com.au. Mains $18–$33. AE, DC, MC, V. Lunch & dinner daily. Train: Central. Map p 92.*

★★★ **Marque** SURRY HILLS *FRENCH* The simple dining room belies the complexity of the food, with its focus on molecular gastronomy. The chef is a culinary wizard, and a meal here is nothing short of a performance. It's degustation-only, but Friday lunch is the best bargain in the city; three courses for just $45. *355 Crown St.* ☎ *02/9332 2225. www.marquerestaurant.com. au. 8 courses $150. AE, DC, MC, V.*

*Lunch Fri, dinner Mon–Sat. Bus: 378, 380. Map p 95.*

**Mezzaluna** POTTS POINT *ITALIAN* Classy classic northern Italian food with great views of the city skyline. *123 Victoria St.* ☎ *02/9357 1988. www.mezzaluna.com.au. Mains $24–$43. AE, DC, MC, V. Lunch Fri, dinner Mon–Sat. Train: Kings Cross. Map p 94.*

★★★ **Montpellier Public House** RANDWICK *CONTEMPORARY* Tucked away in suburban Randwick, the former Restaurant Balzac boasts consistently good French and English food and service that makes it well worth the trip. Go upstairs for fine dining, downstairs for much-better-than-average bar food and a fabulous Sunday roast. *141 Belmore Rd.* ☎ *02/9399 9660. www.montpellierpublichouse.com. au. Mains $24–$30. AE, DC, MC, V. Lunch & dinner daily. Bus: 372, 373, 374. Map p 91.*

**North Bondi Italian Food** BONDI *ITALIAN* This is where the young, beautiful, and very cool head to eat. And who can blame them— the food tastes as good as they look. Be prepared to wait; they don't take bookings. *118 Ramsgate*

*The elegant Quay.*

Ave. ☎ 02/9300 4400. www.idrb.com. Mains $18–$33. AE, DC, MC, V. Lunch Fri–Sun, dinner daily. Bus: 380. Map p 91.

**Otto** WOOLLOOMOOLOO *ITALIAN* Swish fine dining with lots of alfresco tables on the wharf. One of the best spots to rub shoulders with celebrities—Russell Crowe owns an apartment on the wharf, and it's a favorite haunt of Hugh Jackman and Nicole Kidman when they are in town. *Shop 8, 6 Cowper Wharf Rd.* ☎ 02/9368 7488. www.otto ristorante.com.au. Mains $39–$44. AE, DC, MC, V. Lunch & dinner daily. Bus: 311. Map p 92.

**Porteno** SURRY HILLS *ARGENTIN-IAN* Argentinian is the flavor of the month in Sydney right now, and the hottest new restaurant in town is Porteno, which dishes up meat, meat, and more meat with rocka-billy flair. Everyone raves about the 8-hour wood-fired suckling pig and lamb. Bookings accepted for groups of five or more only. *358 Cleveland St.* ☎ 02/8399 1440.

www.porteno.com.au. Mains $16–$44. MC, V. Dinner Mon–Sat. Bus: 372. Map p 95.

**★★★ Quay** THE ROCKS *CONTEM-PORARY* If you're searching for some wow factor for a special occasion, head to Quay for very fine dining and an unbeatable view of the Opera House and Harbour Bridge. *Overseas Passenger Terminal.* ☎ 02/9251 5600. www.quay.com.au. 4 courses $165. AE, DC, MC, V. Lunch Tues–Fri, dinner daily. Train: Circular Quay. Map p 92.

**★★ Restaurant Atelier** GLEBE *FRENCH* Stylish French bistro in a historic brick cottage. *22 Glebe Point Rd.* ☎ 02/9566 2112. www.restaurantatelier.com.au. Mains $36. MC, V. Dinner Tues–Sat. Bus: 431, 433. Map p 95.

**★★ Ripples** MILSONS POINT *CON-TEMPORARY* Fantastic little BYO restaurant right under the Harbour Bridge, next door to Luna Park. It's 100% alfresco with great harbor views—and it's half the price of the waterfront eateries on the south side of the bridge. *North Sydney*

*The intimate and lovely Atelier.*

Olympic Pool, Olympic Dr. ☎ 02/9929 7722. www.ripplescafe.com.au. Mains $26–$32. MC, V. Breakfast, lunch, & dinner daily. Train: Milsons Point. Map p 92.

**Rockpool** THE ROCKS SEAFOOD Celebrity chef Neil Perry's restaurant is, as the name suggests, mostly all about fish. Expensive, even by Sydney standards, but it's nice to know that all the fish have been caught using a "minimal stress regime," whatever that may be. 107 George St. ☎ 02/9252 1888. www.rockpool.com. 4 courses $155. AE, DC, MC, V. Dinner Tues–Sat. Train: Circular Quay. Map p 92.

**★★★ Sailors Thai** THE ROCKS THAI Authentic Thai street food dished up in a historic sailor's home. Head downstairs to classic dining, or upstairs to the casual Canteen noodle bar for equally exquisite food at almost half the price, served at a long communal table. An exotic culinary adventure. 106 George St. ☎ 02/9251 2466. www.sailorsthai.com.au. Mains $17–$39. AE, DC, MC, V. Lunch Mon–Fri, dinner Mon–Sat (& Sun at Canteen). Train: Circular Quay. Map p 92.

**★★★ Sean's Panorama** BONDI CONTEMPORARY Don't let the casual cafe looks fool you. Chef Sean Moran produces seriously good food at this great beachside location at the quieter (northern) end of Bondi Beach. Bookings can be hard to get. 270 Campbell Parade. ☎ 02/9365 4924. www.seanspanaroma.com.au. Mains $31–$49. MC, V. Lunch Fri–Sun, dinner Wed–Sat. Bus: 380. Map p 91.

**Spice I Am** SURRY HILLS THAI Cheap as chips and great food to boot. Expect to queue, but once inside, the fiery home-cooked fare is dished out at a fast and furious rate. Strictly BYO. 90 Wentworth St. ☎ 02/9280 0928. www.spiceiam.com. Mains $14–$26. No credit cards. Lunch & dinner Tues–Sun. Train: Central. Map p 95.

**★ kids Sugaroom** PYRMONT CONTEMPORARY Take a seat by the window and watch the harbor at work as tugboats and container ships cruise by. Great prices given the waterfront location. 1 Harris St. ☎ 02/9571 5055. www.sugaroom.com.au. Mains $28–$39. AE, DC, MC, V. Lunch Tues–Sun, dinner Mon–Sat. Bus: 443, 449. Map p 92.

**★★ kids Swell** BRONTE CONTEMPORARY Casual beachside cafe perfect for a leisurely brunch or lunch; at night it's more formal and hard to beat on a balmy summer evening. 465 Bronte Rd. ☎ 02/9386 5001. www.swellrestaurant.com.au. Breakfast $7–$18, mains $28–$32. AE, MC, V. Breakfast & lunch daily, dinner Wed–Sun. Bus: 378. Map p 91.

**kids Sydney Tower Buffet** CITY CENTER CONTEMPORARY It's all about the view at this revolving restaurant, so if you are looking to spend money on seriously good food, you might be better off going

*In the old CSR Sugar plant is Sugaroom*

*Modern twists on Indian classics at Zaaffran.*

elsewhere. *Gallery Level, 100 Market St. ☎ 02/8223 3800. www.trippas whitegroup.com.au. Set price $50–$85 adults, $25 kids. AE, MC, V. Lunch & dinner daily. Map p 92.*

★★★ **Tetsuyas** CITY CENTER *JAPANESE/FRENCH* If you're lucky enough to get in to this world-renowned restaurant, prepare to be blown away by the 10-course set menu of inspired French and Japanese dishes. It's regularly on the lists of the world's top-10 restaurants. Bookings are very difficult to get.

*529 Kent St. ☎ 02/9267 2900. www. tetsuyas.com. 10 courses $210. AE, DC, MC, V. Lunch Sat, dinner Tues–Sat. Train: Town Hall. Map p 92.*

**Ventuno Pizzeria Enoteca Birreria** WALSH BAY *ITALIAN* This buzzy but glam restaurant at Walsh Bay dishes up antipasti, pizza, pasta, Italian wines, and boutique Italian beers. Go on Sunday night and have your choice of pizza and a glass of house wine or Italian boutique beer for $25. *21 Hickson Rd. ☎ 02/9247 4444. www.ventuno. com.au. Mains $19–$28. Lunch & dinner daily. Train: Circular Quay. Map p 92.*

**Yoshii** THE ROCKS *JAPANESE* You'll find seriously good sushi and other Japanese culinary wonders at this tiny restaurant, with just enough room for 40, hidden away in The Rocks. Choice of two set menus only. *115 Harrington St. ☎ 02/9247 2566. www.yoshii.com.au. 12-course set menu $130–$140. AE, DC, MC, V. Lunch Mon–Sat, dinner daily. Train: Circular Quay. Map p 92.*

**Zaaffran** DARLING HARBOUR *INDIAN* It can be difficult to find good Indian food in Sydney, so thank goodness for Zaaffran. Ignore the mall that surrounds it and concentrate instead on the glittering city skyline view and the delicious food. *Level 2, 345 Harbourside Shopping Centre. ☎ 02/9211 8900. www.zaaffran.com. Mains $18–$40. AE, DC, MC, V. Lunch & dinner daily. Light Rail/Monorail: Convention. Map p 92.* ●

# Nightlife **Best Bets**

Best Celebrity Spotting
★★ Zeta, *Level 4, 488 George St.*
*(p 114)*

Best Cocktails
★★★ Arthouse Hotel, *275 Pitt St.*
*(p 111)*

Best Drag Shows
★★ Imperial Hotel, *35 Erskineville*
*Rd. (p 118)*

Best Dressed Crowd
★★★ Hugos Lounge, *Level 1,*
*33 Bayswater Rd. (p 115)*

Best Place to Get Rich Quick
The Star, *80 Pyrmont St. (p 114)*

Best Girls' Night Out
★★★ The Victoria Room, *Level 1,*
*235 Victoria St. (p 114)*

Most Historic Pub
★★ Fortune of War, *137 George St.*
*(p 117);* and ★★★ The Lord Nelson,
*19 Kent St. (p 117)*

Best Jazz
★★★ The Basement, *29 Reiby*
*Place (p 114)*

Best Microbrewery
★★★ The Lord Nelson, *19 Kent St.*
*(p 117)*

Most Opulent Bar
★★★ Marble Bar, *Level B1, 488*
*George St. (p 113)*

Best People-Watching
★★★ Ravesi's, *Corner Campbell*
*Parade & Hall St. (p 113)*

Best Place to Meet Prince
Charming
★★ Slip Inn, *111 Sussex St. (p 117)*

Best Pub Rock
★ Annandale Hotel, *17 Parramatta*
*Rd. (p 114)*

Best Small Bar
★★★ Love Tilly Devine, *91 Crown*
*Lane (p 112)*

Best View
★★★ Blu Bar on 36, *176 Cumber-*
*land St. (p 111);* and ★★★ Opera
Bar, *Lower Concourse level, Sydney*
*Opera House (p 113)*

*Chinese Laundry Lounge is a sleek nightclub hidden beneath the Slip Inn.*

# Inner West Nightlife

Annandale Hotel 1
Bank Hotel 3
Imperial Hotel 4
Kuleto's 6
Landsdowne Hotel 8
Madame Fling Flong 5
The Sly Fox 2
The Vanguard 7

**EVELEIGH**

Park St
Clara St
Henderson Rd
Swanson St

**CityRail Stop**
**Hospital**

0      1/4 mi
0      0.25 km

**ERSKINEVILLE**

Charles St
Prospect St
Rochford St
Union St
Gowrie St
Angel St

**MACDONALDTOWN**

Burren St

THE UNIVERSITY
OF SYDNEY

City Rd
Darlington Rd

**DARLINGTON**

Rose St
Abercrombie St
Wilson Ln
Forbes St
Queen St
Wilson St
Fitzroy St

Western Ave

Alfred Hospital
King George V
Memorial Hospital

Carillon Ave
Campbell St
King St
Missenden Rd
Susan St
O'Connell St

Bucknell St
Watkin St

**NEWTOWN**

Wilson St
King St
Erskineville Rd
Thomas St

Hordern St
Church St

Camperdown
Memorial
Rest Park

Lennox St
King St

Australia St
Denison St
Probert St
Bedford St

Bailey St
Station St
King St

Lucas St
Grose St
Church St
Mallett St

Northwood St
Roberts St
Hopetoun St
Salisbury Rd
Federation Rd
Abermarle St
Bishopgate St

Enmore Rd

Australia St
Denison St

O'Dea
Reserve

Marmion Rd
Kingston Rd
Salisbury Rd

Gladstone St
London St
Cambridge St
Liberty St

**ENMORE**

Cardigan St
Bridge Rd

Rosevear St
Railway Ave
Trafalgar St
Harrow Rd
Cambridge St
Cavendish St
Stanmore Rd

Parramatta Rd
Corunna Rd
Macauley Rd
Albany Rd

*Photo p 105: Mixologist at the Rum Diaries.*

# Inner Sydney Nightlife

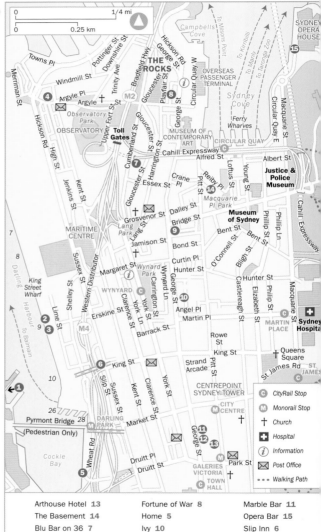

| | | |
|---|---|---|
| Arthouse Hotel 13 | Fortune of War 8 | Marble Bar 11 |
| The Basement 14 | Home 5 | Opera Bar 15 |
| Blu Bar on 36 7 | Ivy 10 | Slip Inn 6 |
| Cargo Bar 2 | The Loft 3 | The Star 1 |
| Establishment Bar 9 | The Lord Nelson 4 | Zeta 12 |

# Eastern Suburbs Nightlife

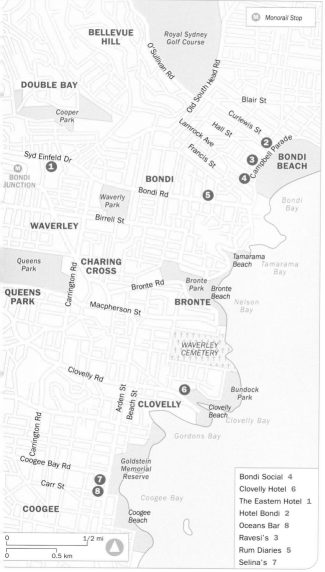

Bondi Social 4
Clovelly Hotel 6
The Eastern Hotel 1
Hotel Bondi 2
Oceans Bar 8
Ravesi's 3
Rum Diaries 5
Selina's 7

# Kings Cross Nightlife

| | |
|---|---|
| 0 | 1/8 mi |
| 0 | 0.125 km |

**C** CityRail Stop
**i** Information
**···** Walking Path

POTTS
POINT

ART GALLERY
OF NEW
SOUTH WALES

Bland St
Nicholson St
Wilson St
Plunkett St
Griffiths St
Harmer St

Stephen St

WOOLLOOMOOLOO

Cathedral St

KINGS
CROSS

Turner Ln

William Ln

William St

Bayswater Rd

**4** **5** Kings Cross Rd
KINGS
CROSS
entrance to
Cross City Tunnel

Stanley St
Chapel St

DARLINGHURST

Liverpool Ln
Liverpool St
Kings Ln

Liverpool St

Burton St

Green
Park

Oxford St

Campbell St

St Neot Ave
McDonald Ln
Challis Ave

Cowper Wharf Rd

Hughes St
Orwell St

Greenknowe A

Craigend S

| |  |
|---|---|
| Eau De Vie | 2 |
| Hugo's Lounge | 6 |
| Kings Cross Hotel | |
| Love Tilly Devine | 1 |
| The Piano Room | 5 |
| The Victoria Room | |

# Inner South Nightlife

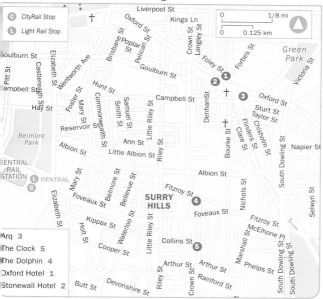

CityRail Stop

Light Rail Stop

Arq 3
The Clock 5
The Dolphin 4
Oxford Hotel 1
Stonewall Hotel 2

# Sydney Nightlife A to Z

### Bars & Lounges

★★★ **Arthouse Hotel** CITY CEN-
TER The beautifully refurbished
1830s School of Arts is now the
place to go for clever cocktails.
There are four bars, with DJs, jazz,
and lots of original art. *275 Pitt St.*
☎ *02/9284 1200. Train: Town Hall.
Map p 108.*

★★★ **Blu Bar on 36** THE ROCKS
Drink in the glorious city, harbor,
and Opera House views at this swish
bar on the 36th floor of the Shangri-
La Hotel. It's very grown-up and
sophisticated, so be at your best
dressed. *176 Cumberland St.*
☎ *02/9250 6000. Train: Circular
Quay. Map p 108.*

★★★ **Bondi Social** BONDI
Secure a table on the balcony overlooking Bondi Beach and throw back
a mojito or two during happy hour
(Tues–Fri 6–7pm, Sat 4–7pm, all
night Sun). They also do great food
(p 97). *Level 1, 38 Campbell Parade.*
☎ *02/9365 1788. Bus: 380. Map
p 109.*

**Cargo Bar** KING STREET WHARF
You'll find a mixed, mainly under-40
crowd here, drawn to the Darling
Harbour view. Gets a bit frantic on
Friday nights, so head to the courtyard if you want to hear yourself
think. *52–60 The Promenade.*
☎ *02/9262 1777. Train: Wynyard.
Map p 108.*

*Blu Bar on 36.*

★★★ **Eau De Vie** DARLINGHURST Hidden away at the back of the Kirketon Hotel (head through the doors marked "restroom") this dark and moody speak-easy-style bar is the perfect place for a secret assignation. Not one for wine lovers (although they offer a few wines), the menu is all about cocktails and quality booze. *229 Darlinghurst Rd.* ☎ *02/9357 2470. Train: Kings Cross. Map p 110.*

**Establishment Bar** CITY CENTER Cavernous space that fills with suits after work, and hip young things as the night wears on. Tuesday nights are rumba nights with a free dance lesson before the party kicks off at 8pm. *252 George St.* ☎ *02/9240 3000. Train: Wynyard. Map p 108.*

**Ivy** CITY CENTER A theme park for cool and beautiful grown-ups with more restaurants, bars, cocktail lounges, and live music venues than you count after one or two of their cocktails. *320–330 George St.* ☎ *02/9240 3000. Train: Wynyard. Map p 108.*

★★ **Kuleto's** NEWTOWN Buy one, get one (the same one) free at this popular little cocktail bar

(during happy hour on weekdays 6–7:30pm and Sat 6–7pm). *157 King St.* ☎ *02/9519 6369. Train: Newtown. Map p 107.*

**The Loft** KING STREET WHARF Gorgeous lounge reminiscent of a Moorish casbah with views over Darling Harbour. *3 Lime St.* ☎ *02/9299 4770. Train: Wynyard. Map p 108.*

★★★ **Love Tilly Devine** DARLINGHURST Secret Sydney at its best. It can be tricky to find this tiny little laneway bar named after one of Sydney's most notorious female gangsters, and even trickier to get in—there's only room for 40—but the wine list is terrific and service is great. 91 Crown Lane. ☎ *02/9326 9297. Train: Kings Cross. Map p 110.*

★ **Madame Fling Flong** NEWTOWN It's hard to leave this great little cocktail bar if you've managed to score yourself a spot on the couch. It's tiny, and fills up quickly, but it feels just like your lounge room at home, especially on movie nights, only with much better drinks. *Upstairs, 169 King St.* ☎ *02/9565 2471. Train: Newtown. Map p 107.*

★★★ **Marble Bar** CITY CENTER
A subterranean work of art in the Italian Renaissance style with Corinthian columns, lots of bronze and stained glass, and 100 tonnes (35 varieties) of multicolored marble, built in 1893. Live music Wednesday to Saturday. *Level B1, 488 George St. (under the Hilton Hotel).* ☎ *02/ 9265 6026. Train: Town Hall. Map p 108.*

★ **Oceans Bar** COOGEE    A rare touch of style in beachfront Coogee. Go here if you want something more than a cold beer or raucous rock. Good pizzas and snacks, and happy hour is every night from 5 to 7pm. *242 Arden St.* ☎ *02/9315 9178. Bus: 372, 373, 374. Map p 109.*

★★★ **Opera Bar** CIRCULAR QUAY
Sophisticated Sydney at its best. Grab an outside table and soak up one of the most spectacular views in town. Lower Concourse level, Sydney Opera House. ☎ *02/9247 1666. Train: Circular Quay. Map p 108.*

**The Piano Room** KINGS CROSS
Sophisticated piano bar above the iconic neon Coke sign. It's gorgeous,

*Marble Bar.*

but the cocktails are on the pricey side. *Corner Kings Cross & Darlinghurst roads.* ☎ *02/9326 0633. Train: Kings Cross. Map p 110.*

★★★ **Ravesi's** BONDI    The downstairs bar with floor-to-ceiling windows is a great perch for people-watching, while Drift, the upstairs bar overlooking the beach,

*The Opera Bar offers picture-perfect views of Harbour Bridge.*

*High tea at the Victoria Room Bar & Restaurant.*

is a more sophisticated spot. *Corner Campbell Parade & Hall St.* ☎ *02/ 9365 4422. Bus: 380. Map p 109.*

★★★ **Rum Diaries** BONDI  There are more rum cocktails on the menu than a drunken sailor can count at this little hideaway bar, but also plenty of good wine, nonrum drinks, and a great snack menu with share-able plates. Don't be put off by the shop-front exterior—it's lovely inside. *288 Bondi Rd.* ☎ *02/9300 0440. Bus: 380. Map p 109.*

★★★ **The Victoria Room** DARLINGHURST  Bordello chic, although they prefer to describe it as British-Raj. Either way, think red velvet, gilt edges, and rich wallpa-pers. Popular with gal-pals who flock here for a sophisticated high tea in the afternoon and cocktails once the sun sets. The bar snacks are a little uninspired though.

*Level 1, 235 Victoria St.* ☎ *02/9357 4488. Bus: 311. Map p 110.*

★★ **Zeta** CITY CENTER  Sexy and sleek—which is also the best way to describe the crowd. Seems visiting celebrities like Jessica Simpson, Nicky Hilton, Nicole Richie, Megan Gale, and Hugh Jackman, who have all enjoyed a tipple or two here, agree. *Hilton Hotel, Level 4, 488 George St.* ☎ *02/9265 6070. Train: Town Hall. Map p 108.*

## Casino

**The Star** PYRMONT  Sydney's only (legal) casino has all the requi-site ways to lose (or win) money, with 200 gaming tables and more pokies (slot machines) than you can count. There are nine bars and clubs in the complex, 12 restaurants, and it's open all night if you're planning a big one. *80 Pyrmont St.* ☎ *02/ 9777 9000. www.star.com.au. Light rail: Star City. Monorail: Harbour-side. Map p 108.*

## Live Music & Dance Clubs

★ **Annandale Hotel** ANNAN-DALE  Expect everything from reggae to heavy metal at this working-class pub that's a favorite with students. This is where you'll see the next big thing on stage, Wednesday through Sunday. *17 Parramatta Rd.* ☎ *02/9550 1078. Tickets about $20. Bus: 470. Map p 107.*

★★★ **The Basement** CIRCULAR QUAY  An Australian music land-mark since the 1970s and Sydney's premier jazz and roots music venue with great live music—from home and away—every night of the week. The food's ordinary to awful, but ordering some is a great way to secure a front row seat (it's usually standing room only once the shows start) *29 Reiby Place.*

☎ 02/9251 2797. www.the basement.com.au. Ticket prices vary. Train: Circular Quay. Map p 108.

**The Eastern Hotel** BONDI JUNCTION If the weekend seems too far away, head to the delightfully bordello-ish Ruby Lounge or the rooftop Pacifica on a Wednesday night for a mix of R & B, electro-pop, and house. *500 Oxford St.* ☎ *02/9387 7828. Entry: free to about $10. Train: Bondi Junction. Map p 109.*

**Home** DARLING HARBOUR Burn up the floor until the sun comes up in Sydney's largest nightclub. Check the website for details on special events. *101 Cockle Bay Wharf.* ☎ *02/9266 0600. www.home sydney.com. Tickets $15 to $55. Train: Town Hall. Map p 108.*

**★★★ Hugos Lounge** KINGS CROSS Favorite party spot for the in-crowd, so dress to impress or you won't get in. Love the ceiling covered in dozens of mirror balls. *Level 1, 33 Bayswater Rd.* ☎ *02/9357 4411. http://www.hugos.com.au.*

Entry $5 and up. Train: Kings Cross. Map p 110.

**★ Lansdowne Hotel** CHIPPENDALE Good pub. Cheap food. Free bands. What's left to say? Okay, it is a little dark and grimy, and the floor can get a bit sticky—but when it's dark and crowded you hardly notice. Friday and Saturday are the nights to catch some great indie rock played loud. *2 City Rd.* ☎ *02/ 9211 2325. Free entry most nights. Bus: 426, 428, 431, 438, 440, 461. Map p 107.*

**Selina's** COOGEE The Coogee Bay Hotel can get a bit rough and dangerous at times, but it's the biggest nightclub in the eastern suburbs, which means it has the space to host some great names in music as well as good local DJs. The beer garden is a great place to be on a summer afternoon, although it can be overrun with backpackers. *Corner Coogee Bay Rd. & Arden St.* ☎ *02/9665 0000. Prices vary. Bus: 372, 373. Map p 109.*

Basement nightlife.

# Mardi Gras

The world's most glamorous civil rights demonstration started as a protest rally in 1978. It resulted in more than 50 arrests and has grown into one of the world's great LGBT festivals that draws in thousands of fabulously and extravagantly costumed marchers (pictured) as well as huge crowds of cheering spectators of all sexual persuasions each February/March. The main parade route is up Oxford Street, and affiliated events include the Sleaze Ball, countless parties, a gay film festival, concerts, and art shows. Check out www.mardigras.org.au for information about next year's event.

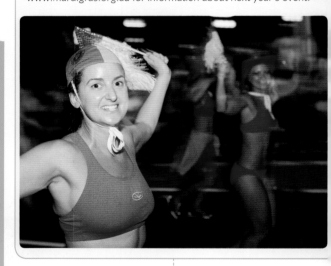

★★ **The Vanguard** NEWTOWN Eclectic lineup of live music, occasionally jazz or blues, but more often local R & B legends or up-and-coming artists, in a dinner/show venue inspired by the great jazz and blues restaurants of New Orleans. *42 King St.* ☎ *02/9557 7992. www. thevanguard.com.au. Tickets $18 to $114. Train: Newtown. Map p 107.*

## Pubs
★★ **Bank Hotel** NEWTOWN Inner-city Newtown has always attracted a mixed crowd of pleasure-seekers, and so does the Bank Hotel, whether it's locals having an after-work beer in the public bar, sleek young things enjoying a cocktail in the lounge, or happy diners tucking into duck curry at the Sumalee Thai restaurant in the courtyard. *324 King St.* ☎ *02/8565 1900. Train: Newtown. Map p 107.*

★★ **The Clock** SURRY HILLS Twenty-something hipsters upstairs; fashionable 30-somethings downstairs; and locals, artists, and musicians mix over the pool tables. *470 Crown St.* ☎ *02/9331 5333. Bus: 310, 302. Map p 111.*

★★★ **Clovelly Hotel** CLOVELLY Not so much a nightspot as a great place to spend Sunday afternoon in the beer garden looking out over the ocean. Very relaxed, very Sydney, this is where famous footballers go to get caught out with their teammates' wives. *381 Clovelly Rd.* ☎ *02/9665 1214. Bus: 339. Map p 109.*

★★★ **The Dolphin** SURRY HILLS A favorite with locals who meet here for drinks, pool, or a (reasonably) cheap meal. It manages to be casually stylish and comfortable at the same time. *412 Crown St.* ☎ *02/9331 4800. Bus: 378, 380. Map p 111.*

★★ **Fortune of War** THE ROCKS Proudly boasting that it's the oldest pub in Sydney, this cozy and atmospheric little pub has a heritage-listed hamper style bar, old-fashioned tiled walls, and jazz on Sunday afternoons. *137 George St.* ☎ *02/9247 2714. Train: Circular Quay. Map p 108.*

**Hotel Bondi** BONDI Great location right on Bondi Beach, but it's all a bit '90s. Popular among backpackers, night owls, and pool sharks who flock to the Sand Bar pool hall. *178 Campbell Parade.* ☎ *02/9130 3271. Bus: 380. Map p 109.*

**Kings Cross Hotel** KINGS CROSS Six sleek and chic levels, a different bar-cum-lounge on each. The Roof Top bar on level five offers great cocktails with a view. *248 William St.* ☎ *02/9331 9900. Train: Kings Cross. Map p 110.*

★★★ **The Lord Nelson** THE ROCKS Also proudly boasting that it's the oldest pub in Sydney. There are quite a few "oldest pubs

in Sydney"; the detail's in the fine print.) The Lord Nelson brews up its own (very good) beer. If you like your beer to pack a punch, try the Old Admiral. *19 Kent St.* ☎ *02/9251 4044. Train: Circular Quay. Map p 108.*

★★ **Slip Inn** CITY CENTER It was just a haunt for the after-work office crowd until real-estate agent Mary Donaldson met her prince charming (Prince Frederik, Crown Prince of Denmark) here. Now it's full of pretty young things hoping to snare a prince for themselves. The underground Chinese Laundry nightclub is worth a look just for the quirky decor. *111 Sussex St. (corner King St.).* ☎ *02/8295 9999. Train: Wynyard. Map p 108.*

### Gay & Lesbian

**Arq** DARLINGHURST Ditch your shirt and party hard with the fierce and fabulous in the biggest gay club in town. *16 Flinders St.* ☎ *02/9380 8700. Bus: 378, 380. Map p 111.*

*The Lord Nelson.*

---

Drag queen at the Imperial.

**★★ Imperial Hotel** ERSKINE-VILLE   Priscilla, eat your heart out. Hilarious drag shows and a huge underground dance floor. Everyone's always happy here. *35 Erskineville Rd. ☎ 02/9519 9899. Train: Newtown. Map p 107.*

**Oxford Hotel** DARLINGHURST All-nighter that can get sleazy at 7am on a Sunday. Popular with guys aged 30 to 50—of all types—when the sun goes down. *134 Oxford St. ☎ 02/9181 1229. Bus: 378, 380. Map p 111.*

**The Sly Fox** ENMORE   Pop by for Tuesday night Bingay, a hilarious and naughty version of the old folks' favorite game, which—here—is hosted by drag queens and raises funds for the Aids Council of NSW. *199 Enmore Rd. ☎ 02/9557 1016. Train: Newtown. Map p 107.*

**Stonewall Hotel** DARLINGHURST Something for everyone no matter what your taste with DJs, drag performances, male dancers, and live entertainment 7 nights a week. Expect a youngish and enthusiastic crowd. *175 Oxford St. ☎ 02/9360 1963. Bus: 378, 380. Map p 111.* ●

*The Vanguard hosts an eclectic array of musical performances.*

# Arts & Entertainment **Best Bets**

Best **Acoustics**
★★ City Recital Hall, *Angel Place* (p 126)

Best **Art House Movies**
★★ Palace Verona, *17 Oxford St.* (p 128)

Best **Australian Drama**
★★★ Belvoir St. Theatre, *25 Belvoir St.* (p 129)

Best **Belly Laughs**
Sydney Comedy Store, *Lang Rd.* (p 126)

Best **Free Show**
★★★ Domain Concert Series, *The Domain (below)*

Best **Modern Dance**
Sydney Dance Company, *at either Sydney Theatre, 22 Hickson Rd.* (p 130), or the Opera House, Bennelong Point (p 127)

Most **Opulent Surrounds**
★★★ State Theatre, *49 Market St.* (p 128)

Best **Peek Backstage**
★★★ Backstage tour at the Sydney Opera House, *Bennelong Point* (p 127)

Best **Playwrights You've Never Heard Of**
★★ SBW Stables Theatre, *10 Nimrod St.* (p 130)

Best **Under the Stars**
★★★ Moonlight Cinema, *Centennial Park (p 124)*

## Under the Stars

Why lock yourself indoors when you can be out enjoying the best of a ★★★ balmy Sydney summer night under the stars? During the summer there's a whole range of outdoor theaters, concerts, and movies that take advantage of Sydney's glorious weather and fabulous parklands. In January there's the **Domain Concert Series,** with free opera, classical music, and jazz concerts in the Domain as part of the annual **Sydney Festival** (www.sydneyfestival. org.au). Catch the latest movies and some cult classics on a big outdoor screen at the **OpenAir Cinema** in the Royal Botanic Gardens (map p 122) mid-January to mid-February (www.stgeorgeopenair. com.au). The **Moonlight Cinema** in Centennial Park (map p 124), which kicks off in November and runs through to March, is a much more casual affair. Bring a blanket and a picnic or hire a beanbag for $6 and buy food and wine there (www.moonlight.com.au).

# Inner West A&E

Carriageworks **4**
Enmore Theatre **5**
Friend in Hand Hotel **1**
New Theatre **6**
King Street Theatre **7**
Roxbury Hotel **2**
Seymour Centre **3**

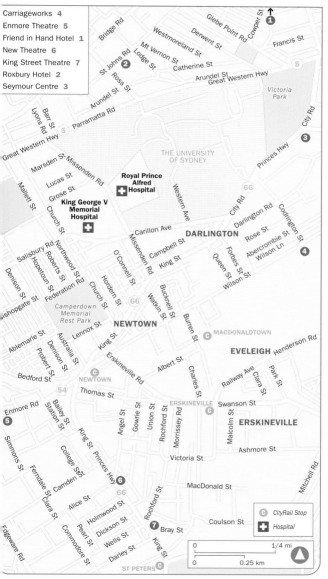

# Inner Sydney A&E

**C** CityRail Stop
**L** Light Rail Stop
**M** Monorail Stop
**†** Church
**✚** Hospital
**(i)** Information
**✉** Post Office
**- - -** Walking Path

Sydney Harbour Bridge
DAWES POINT
Daw Poi Par
THE ROCKS
Walsh Bay
Towns Pl
HARBOUR CONTROL TOWER
Windmill St
Hickson Rd
Bradfield Hwy
Trinity Ave
Lower Fort St
Hickson Rd
George St
Merriman St
MILLERS POINT
Argyle
Observatory Park
OBSERVATORY
Cumberland St
Harrington St
Cahill Expressw
Toll Gates
Gloucester St
Crane
Darling St BALMAIN EAST
Johnston St
William St
Union St
Illoura Reserve
Peacock Point
Hickson Rd
Kent St
Jenkins St
Dalley
Bridge
Johnstons Bay
Darling Harbour
MARITIME CENTRE
Lang Park
Jamison St
Bond
Sussex St
Margaret St
Carrington St
George St
DARLING ISLAND PASSENGER TERMINAL 13
SYDNEY PASSENGER TERMINAL
King Street Wharf
Shelley St
Erskine St
WYNYARD **C**
Barrack St
Pirrama Rd
Point St
Lime St
Clarence St
Kent St
York St
George St
STAR CITY **L**
Pyrmont Ferry 10
Pyrmont Bay Park
King St
Sussex St
Ship St
JOHN STREET SQUARE **L**
Bowman St
Harris St
Mount St
Miller St
Pyrmont St
PYRMONT BAY **L**
AUSTRALIAN NATIONAL MARITIME MUSEUM
SYDNEY AQUARIUM
Clarence St
Market St
PYRMONT
HARBOURSIDE
Union St
Darling Dr
Pyrmont Bridge (Pedestrian Only)
Cockle Bay
DARLING PARK
Druitt Pl
Druitt St
FISHMARKET **L**
Experiment St
Harris St
Murray St
Pyrmont St
HARBOURSIDE FESTIVAL MARKETPLACE
CONVENTION **L M**
Wheat Rd
Day St
Bathurst S
Allen St
SYDNEY CONVENTION CENTRE
Blackwattle Bay
Bulwara Rd
Jones St
Fig St
Ada Pl
DARLING HARBOUR
SYDNEY EXHIBITION CENTRE
Tumbalong Park
Chinese Gardens
Liverpool St
GARDEN PLAZA **M**
Sussex St
Dixon St
WENTWORTH PARK **L**
Bridge Rd
Wattle St
Quarry St
Darling Dr
EXHIBITION CENTRE **L**
Pier St
THE POWERHOUSE MUSEUM
Harbour St
Daggahan St
Bellevue St
Wentworth Park Rd
ULTIMO
PADDY'S MARKETS
CAPITOL SQUARE

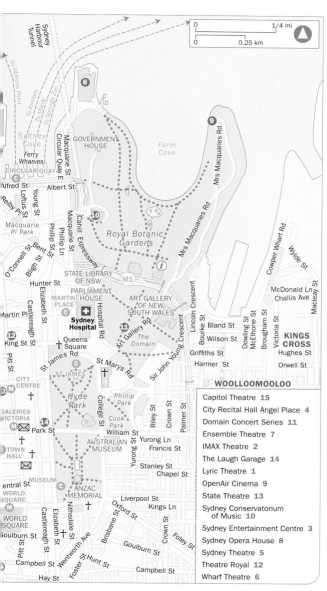

Capitol Theatre **15**
City Recital Hall Angel Place **4**
Domain Concert Series **11**
Ensemble Theatre **7**
IMAX Theatre **2**
The Laugh Garage **14**
Lyric Theatre **1**
OpenAir Cinema **9**
State Theatre **13**
Sydney Conservatorium
   of Music **10**
Sydney Entertainment Centre **3**
Sydney Opera House **8**
Sydney Theatre **5**
Theatre Royal **12**
Wharf Theatre **6**

124

## The Best Arts & Entertainment

# Inner East A&E

Belvoir St Theatre **1**
Comedy Store **8**
Darlinghurst Theatre **7**
Govinda's **3**
Moonlight Cinema **9**
Old Fitzroy Theatre **2**
Palace Verona **4**
Parade Theatres **6**
SBW Stables Theatre **5**

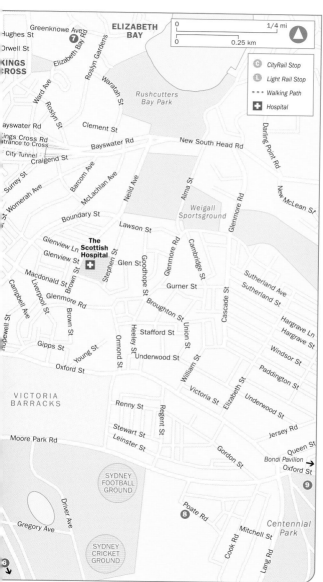

# Sydney A&E A to Z

## Classical Music

### ★★ City Recital Hall Angel Place CITY CENTER
Tucked away in a tiny laneway, this is the place to go if you like classical music. Designed in a shoebox shape (apparently the best shape for listening to Western classical music), this is the home of the city's best orchestras. It's flash, so dress up. *2 Angel Place (btw. George & Pitt sts. near Martin Place).* ☎ *02/8256 2222. www.city recitalhall.com. Ticket prices vary. Train: Martin Place. Map p 122.*

### Sydney Conservatorium of Music CITY CENTER
Part of the University of Sydney, the Conservatorium is one of the country's most prestigious music schools. See the classical stars of tomorrow for much less than the ticket price of a concert elsewhere. *Macquarie St. (opposite Bridge St.).* ☎ *02/8256 2222. www. music.usyd.edu.au. Ticket prices vary. Train: Circular Quay. Map p 122.*

*Improv at the Roxbury Hotel.*

## Comedy

### Friend in Hand Hotel GLEBE
See the best up-and-coming comedians on stage every Thursday at 7:30pm. If you're really lucky, you might even catch some high-profile acts trying out their new material, a dirt-cheap preview to next year's big comedy show. *58 Cowper St.* ☎ *02/ 9660 2326. www.amicinhand.com. Tickets $10. Bus: 431, 433. Map p 121.*

### The Laugh Garage CITY CENTER
One of the few comedy clubs in the city, it has a (usually) good lineup of local stand-up acts Wednesday through Saturday. *Corner Elizabeth & Park sts.* ☎ *02/9264 1161. www. thelaughgarage.com. Tickets $12– $25. Train: Town Hall. Map p 122.*

### Roxbury Hotel GLEBE
There's comedy on stage here almost every night of the week, but Wednesday night has some of the best improvised theater and comedy around. *182 St. Johns Rd.* ☎ *02/9692 0822. www.roxbury.com.au. Tickets $15. Bus: 431, 433. Map p 121.*

### Sydney Comedy Store MOORE PARK
One of Sydney's few dedicated comedy venues features a good lineup of both local and international talent as well as up-and-coming amateurs. Closed Sunday and Monday. *Entertainment Quarter, Building 207/122 Lang Rd.* ☎ *02/9357 1419. www.comedystore.com.au. Tickets $10–$30. Bus: 372–377, 290–399 from Circular Quay. Map p 124.*

## Contemporary Arts

### Carriageworks REDFERN
The old railway sheds have been transformed into a contemporary arts center with theater spaces and galleries. Sydney Dance Company regularly performs here, as do other contemporary dance companies,

*The Carriageworks galleries.*

and there's usually some weird and wonderful installation art. It's a rough area, so opt for a taxi after the show. *245 Wilson St.* ☎ *02/8571 9099. www.carriageworks.com.au. Ticket prices vary. Train: Redfern. Map p 121.*

### Movies

**Govinda's** DARLINGHURST Dine on the gourmet vegetarian buffet then retire upstairs and lay back on the cushions at the comfiest movie house in town. Just be careful you don't fall asleep. *112 Darlinghurst Rd.* ☎ *02/9380 5155. www.govindas. com.au. Tickets $14. Train: Kings Cross. Map p 124.*

**IMAX Theatre** DARLING HARBOUR If you believe bigger is better you'll love this screen that's 10 times the size of a traditional cinema screen.

## Sydney Opera House

No visit to Sydney is complete without a visit to the city's most famous building, the ★★★ **Sydney Opera House.** The World Heritage–listed building has seven performance venues, and on average "the House" puts on more than 1,500 performances in front of almost 1.3 million people each year, making it one of the world's busiest performing arts centers.

Aside from seeing a show (such as Massive Attack, pictured below), there are a number of tours, including a 1-hour history and heritage Essential Tour (tickets $28–$35) and the excellent early morning 2-hour Backstage Tour, which might well be your only chance to sing on stage ($150 including breakfast in the Green Room).

Trivia buffs: The first person to perform at the House was Paul Robeson, who climbed the scaffolding and sang "Ol' Man River" to the construction workers as they ate their lunch in 1960.

The Best Arts & Entertainment

Kids love the regular 3-D screenings. *31 Wheat Rd.* ☎ *02/9281 3300. www.imax.com.au. Tickets $15–$20. Monorail: Darling Park. Map p 122.*

★★ **Palace Verona** PADDINGTON The best place to go if you're looking for quality art house and foreign movies. Monday is discount day and all sessions are $11. *17 Oxford St.* ☎ *02/9360 6099. www.palace cinemas.com.au. Tickets $14–$18. Bus: 378 from Central or 380 from Circular Quay. Map p 124.*

### Song & Dance
★★ **Capitol Theatre** HAYMARKET This beautifully restored 1928 theater is the place to catch the latest blockbuster musical. The ceiling of the auditorium reflects the stars in the southern winter sky, as mapped by the Sydney Observatory. *13 Campbell St. (btw. George & Pitt sts.).* ☎ *02/9320 5000. www.capitol theatre.com.au. Tickets $45–$110. Train: Central. Map p 122.*

**Enmore Theatre** NEWTOWN This Art Deco theater is mainly a contemporary music venue, but it occasionally features off-the-wall comedy and musicals. *132 Enmore Rd. (near Simmons St.).* ☎ *02/9550 3666. www.enmoretheatre.com.au.*

*Ticket prices vary. Train: Newtown. Map p 121.*

★ **Lyric Theatre** PYRMONT One of the city's few purpose-built theaters, the huge stage is great for big-budget productions. Program runs from musicals and theater to opera and ballet. *The Star, 80 Pyrmont St.* ☎ *02/9777 9000; tickets 1300 795 267. www.starcity.com.au. Ticket prices vary. Light rail: Star City. Monorail: Harbourside. Map p 122.*

★★★ **State Theatre** CITY CENTER Sydney's most opulent theater was built in 1929 and is an extravagant mix of Gothic, Italian, and Art Deco design. The former "Palace of Dreams" hosts the annual Sydney Film Festival in June, but mainly features international music acts and cabaret. *49 Market St. (btw. Pitt & George sts.).* ☎ *02/9373 6655; tickets 136 100. www.statetheatre.com. au. Ticket prices vary. Train: Town Hall. Map p 122.*

**Sydney Entertainment Centre** DARLING HARBOUR Sydney's largest venue, but if you want to see the latest international superstars, this is where you'll have to go. *35 Harbour St.* ☎ *02/9320 4200; tickets 1300 883 622. www.sydentcent.com.au. Ticket*

*The Capitol Theatre.*

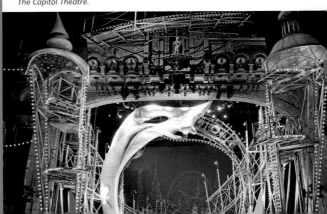

# Sydney Film Festival

Short films, art films, foreign films, documentaries, and screenings—if you're in town in June catch a movie or 20 at the **Sydney Film Festival,** one of the world's longest-running film festivals. The festival is held across a number of Sydney cinemas; see http://www.sff.org.au for program details.

prices vary. Train: Central. Monorail: Paddy's Markets. Map p 122.

**Theatre Royal** CITY CENTER Mainstream megamusicals and dance, but occasionally a little drama, too. *108 King St.* ☎ *02/9224 8444; tickets 132 849. www.theatreroyal. net.au. Ticket prices vary. Train: Martin Place. Map p 122.*

### Theater

**★★★ Belvoir St. Theatre** SURRY HILLS Contemporary and ensemble drama with a focus on hard-edged sometimes radical Australian drama. This is the place to see some of Australia's finest actors on stage. Downstairs is where many Australian playwrights got their first break. *25 Belvoir St.* ☎ *02/9519 3444. www.belvoir.com.au. Tickets $32–$62. Train: Central. Map p 124.*

**Bondi Pavilion** BONDI It's hard to tear yourself away from the sweeping views of Bondi Beach from the balcony, but if you do, you'll be treated to some of the best of Australia's new playwriting talent. *Queen Elizabeth Dr.* ☎ *02/8019 0282. www.rocksurfers.org. Tickets $21–$33. Bus: 280, 389.*

**Darlinghurst Theatre** POTTS POINT Intimate little theater that leans toward the avant-garde with good local talent and first-time productions. *19 Greenknowe Ave.* ☎ *02/8356 9987. www.darlinghurst theatre.com. Tickets $27–$37. Train: Kings Cross. Map p 124.*

**★★ Ensemble Theatre** KIRRI-BILLI A smallish theater with a good lineup of modern classics and Australian drama by the second-longest-running theater company in Australia. The actual theater was once a boatshed and it's worth getting here early to have dinner at the restaurant, which has knockout water views. *78 McDougall St.* ☎ *02/9929 0644. www.ensemble. com.au. Tickets $29–$69. Train: Milsons Point. Map p 122.*

**★ King Street Theatre** NEW-TOWN It's tiny and grungy, but this great 100-seater features the work of emerging playwrights and small independent theater companies. *Corner King & Bray sts.* ☎ *02/9519 5081. www.newtown theatre.com.au. Ticket prices vary. Train: Newtown. Map p 121.*

**New Theatre** NEWTOWN What was once a left-wing political Workers' Theatre established in 1932 is now an independent theater company with an eclectic program, although most works still tend to have a cutting political edge. Good place to catch gay drama. *542 King St.* ☎ *1300 306 776. www.ramin. com.au/online/newtheatre. Tickets $10–$28. Train: Newtown. Map p 121.*

**★★★ Old Fitzroy Theatre** WOOLLOOMOOLOO Hidden away in the back room of a 100-year-old pub, this tiny theater is the home of the Tamarama Rock Surfers, which is dedicated to performing the work

# Rock Festivals

Sydney is host to two major rock festivals each year. The **Big Day Out,** in late January (see below), attracts big name bands from overseas and Australia (see www.bigdayout.com for details, dates, and ticket prices) while **Homebake,** usually in December, features the best of Australian music, with a little Kiwi talent for good measure (see www. homebake.com.au for event details). Both sell out fast, usually months before the event, so get your tickets online before you leave home.

of emerging Australian playwrights. *129 Dowling St.* ☎ *1300 438 849. www.oldfitzroy.com.au. Tickets $20– $28. Train: Kings Cross. Map p 124.*

**Parade Theatres** KENSINGTON Almost all of Australia's acting superstars were trained at the National Institute of Dramatic Art (NIDA). You can catch the next Mel Gibson or Toni Collette at one of the four NIDA Parade theaters. *215 Anzac Parade.* ☎ *02/9697 7600. www.nida.edu.au, click on the "Parade Theatres" tab. Ticket prices vary. Bus: 392, 394, L94, 396, 397, 399 from Circular Quay. Map p 124.*

★★ **SBW Stables Theatre** KINGS CROSS The original home of the Nimrod Theatre and one of the birth-places of contemporary Australian theater. The tradition continues with the resident Griffin Theatre Company, a not-for-profit company committed to emerging playwrights. *10 Nimrod St.* ☎ *1300 306 776. www. griffintheatre.com.au. Tickets $28– $47. Train: Kings Cross. Map p 124.*

★★ **Seymour Centre** CHIPPEN-DALE There are four performance

spaces in this theater on the campus of Sydney University and ticket prices are a good value compared to some other theaters. The new Sound Lounge, formerly a foyer, has jazz on Friday and Saturday nights. *Corner City Rd. & Cleveland St.* ☎ *02/9351 7940. www.seymour.usyd.edu.au. Ticket prices vary. Bus: 422, 423, 426, 428 from Railway Sq. Map p 121.*

★★ **The Wharf & Sydney Theatre** WALSH BAY Home base of the Sydney Theatre Company under the artistic direction of actress Cate Blanchett. An eclectic mix of drama from one-person shows to edgy productions of Shakespeare. There is a third theater opposite Pier 6/7 that stages big-name Australian and international productions. The Wharf makes their own sets and props on-site; behind the scenes tours are held on the first and third Thursdays of each month at 10:30am, and cost $10; bookings essential. *Pier 4/5, Hickson Rd.* ☎ *02/9250 1777. www.sydney theatre.com.au. Ticket prices vary. Bus: 339, 430, 431, 433. Train: Circular Quay. Map p 122.* ●

# 9 The Best **Lodging**

# Lodging **Best Bets**

Best **Bathrooms**
The Westin Sydney $$$$
*1 Martin Place (p 142)*

Best **Beachside Rooms**
★★ Crowne Plaza Hotel $$$
*242 Arden St. (p 136)*

Best **Boutique Hotel**
★ BLUE Sydney $$$$ *6 Cowper Wharf Rd. (p 136)*

Best **for Business**
Fraser Suites Sydney $$$
*488 Kent St. (p 137)*

Best **Bush Escape**
★★★ Lane Cove River Tourist Park $–$$$ *Plassey Rd., North Ryde (p 138)*

Best **Harbor Views**
★★★ Park Hyatt Sydney $$$$$
*7 Hickson Rd. (p 139);* and
★★★ Shangri-La Hotel $$$$
*176 Cumberland St. (p 140)*

Most **Historic Hotel**
★★★ The Grace Hotel $$$ *77 York St. (p 137);* and ★ Q Station $$$ *North Head Scenic Dr. (p 139)*

Best **Kids' Rooms**
★★ Swissôtel Sydney $$$
*68 Market St. (p 140)*

Best **Luxury**
★★★ Park Hyatt Sydney $$$$$
*7 Hickson Rd. (p 139)*

Best **Place to Pretend You're a Local**
★★★ Adina Crown Street $$$ *359 Crown St. (p 136)*

Best **Indoor Pool**
★★★ The Observatory Hotel $$$$$ *89–113 Kent St. (p 138)*

Most **Romantic**
★★★ Hilton Sydney $$$$ *488 George St. (p 137)*

Best **Suites**
The Darling $$$$$ *80 Pyrmont St. (p 136)*

Best **Value**
★★ Hotel Altamont $–$$
*207 Darlinghurst Rd. (p 137);* and
★★★ Sydney Harbour YHA $
*110 Cumberland St. (p 141)*

*Below: The trendy Blu Bar at the lush Shangri-La.*
*Previous page: Blue Sydney Taj Hotel.*

# Eastern Suburbs Lodging

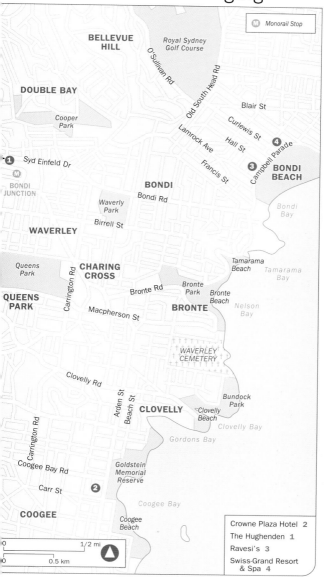

M  Monorail Stop

BELLEVUE HILL

Royal Sydney Golf Course

DOUBLE BAY

O'Sullivan Rd

Old South Head Rd

Blair St

Cooper Park

Curlewis St

Lamrock Ave

Hall St

❹

Syd Einfeld Dr ❶

Francis St

Campbell Parade

M
BONDI JUNCTION

❸  BONDI BEACH

BONDI

Bondi Rd

Bondi Bay

Waverly Park

Birrell St

WAVERLEY

Queens Park

CHARING CROSS

Tamarama Beach

Tamarama Bay

Carrington Rd

Bronte Rd

Bronte Park

Bronte Beach

QUEENS PARK

Macpherson St

BRONTE

Nelson Bay

WAVERLEY CEMETERY

Clovelly Rd

Bundock Park

Arden St

Beach St

CLOVELLY

Clovelly Beach

Clovelly Bay

Gordons Bay

Carrington Rd

Coogee Bay Rd

Goldstein Memorial Reserve

Carr St

❷

Coogee Bay

COOGEE

Coogee Beach

0                    1/2 mi
0          0.5 km

| | |
|---|---|
| Crowne Plaza Hotel | 2 |
| The Hughenden | 1 |
| Ravesi's | 3 |
| Swiss-Grand Resort & Spa | 4 |

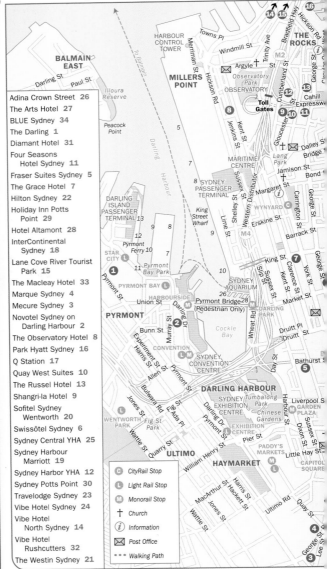

CityRail Stop
Light Rail Stop
Monorail Stop
Church
Information
Post Office
Walking Path

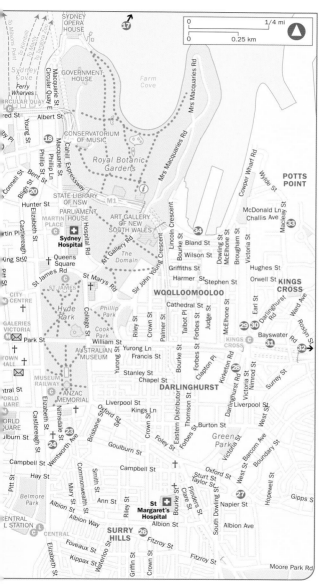

# Sydney **Lodging A to Z**

### ★★★ Adina Crown Street

SURRY HILLS    If you want to live like a local stay at this great value apartment-style hotel in the heart of one of Sydney's best eating and shopping precincts—and only 10 minutes from the city center. *359 Crown St.* ☎ *02/8302 1000. www. medina.com.au. 85 rooms. Doubles $235–$390. AE, DC, MC, V. Bus: 378, 380. Map p 134.*

**The Arts Hotel** PADDINGTON Rooms are a bit uninspired, but it's a good value and in a great location on Oxford Street—particularly if you're a keen shopper. You can often get a discount on the rate below if staying for a few nights. Courtyard rooms are quietest. *21 Oxford St.* ☎ *02/9361 0211. www. artshotel.com.au. 64 rooms. Doubles $185–$210. AE, DC, MC, V. Bus: 378, 380. Map p 134.*

### ★ BLUE Sydney WOOLLOOMO-
OLOO    Boutique hotel on a historic wooden wharf with some split-level loft suites. Easy walk to Botanic Gardens and Opera House. *6 Cowper*

*Wharf Rd.* ☎ *02/9331 9000. www. tajhotels.com/sydney. 100 rooms. Doubles $290–$530. AE, DC, MC, V. Bus: 311. Map p 134.*

### ★★ Crowne Plaza Hotel COOGEE
Coogee Beach is a quieter alternative to the more frenzied and fashionable Bondi, but is also only a few minutes away by bus or taxi. This hotel's opposite the beach so ask for a room with an ocean view. *242 Arden St.* ☎ *1800 007 697. www.ichotels group.com. 209 rooms. Doubles $257–$392. AE, DC, MC, V. Bus: 372, 373, 374. Map p 133.*

**The Darling** DARLING HARBOUR Sydney's newest luxury hotel is worth a splurge. It's part of the Star casino complex, but it has a sepa-rate entrance so it feels a world apart. Rooms are large and very high-tech; most suites have good views over the city and Harbour Bridge. *80 Pyrmont St.* ☎ *1800 800 830. www.thedarling.com.au. 171 rooms. Doubles $399–$1,200. AE, DC, MC, V. Light rail: Star City. Mono-rail: Harbourside. Map p 134.*

*The Adored Suite's modern bathroom, The Darling hotel.*

**★★ Diamant Hotel** POTTS POINT Stylish new boutique hotel in the heart of Kings Cross, although the dark charcoal color scheme in the hallways and rooms can be a bit oppressive. The courtyard rooms have great patios with city views. *14 Kings Cross Rd.* ☎ *02/9295 8888. www.diamant.com.au. 76 rooms. Doubles $195–$325. AE, DC, MC, V. Train: Kings Cross. Map p 134.*

**★★★ Four Seasons Hotel Sydney** THE ROCKS Elegant five-star hotel in an unbeatable location close to The Rocks and the Opera House. Weekend rates are usually cheaper than midweek. *199 George St.* ☎ *02/9238 0000. www.four seasons.com/sydney. 531 rooms. Doubles $290–$645. AE, DC, MC, V. Train: Circular Quay. Map p 134.*

**Fraser Suites Sydney** CITY CENTER This contemporary all-suite hotel is at the Town Hall end of town. A good choice if you're in Sydney on business and need room to spread out. *488 Kent St.* ☎ *1800 800 488. http://sydney.frasers hospitality.com. 201 rooms. Doubles $305–$490. AE, DC, MC, V. Train: Town Hall. Map p 134.*

**★★★ The Grace Hotel** CITY CENTER Beautifully restored 1930s neo-Gothic hotel with gorgeous Art Deco foyer and bar areas. During WWII the hotel was the headquarters of General Douglas MacArthur, who directed the South Pacific operations from here. Weekend rates are usually cheaper than midweek. *77 York St.* ☎ *1800 682 692. www.grace hotel.com.au. 382 rooms. Doubles $220–$380. AE, DC, MC, V. Train: Martin Place. Map p 134.*

**★★★ Hilton Sydney** CITY CENTER Sleek, stylish, and central, the revamped Hilton is one of my favorites. It's got all the gadgets you need if you're working and plenty of wow-factor if it's a special occasion. The naughty-but-nice Provocateur package is guaranteed to provoke passion. You can often get good weekend deals. *488 George St.* ☎ *02/9265 6045. www.hilton sydney.com.au. 577 rooms. Doubles $399–$615. AE, DC, MC, V. Train: Town Hall. Map p 134.*

**★ Holiday Inn Potts Point** KINGS CROSS Good value mid-range hotel close to the action in Kings Cross. Check the website for good package deals. *203 Victoria St.* ☎ *1800 899 960. www.ichotels group.com. 288 rooms. Doubles $248–$345. AE, DC, MC, V. Train: Kings Cross. Map p 134.*

**★★ Hotel Altamont** KINGS CROSS This stylish little hotel used to be a (rather notorious) nightclub and really does offer budget-priced luxury. Rooms are spacious; some of the bathrooms are huge. Favorite is the courtyard room (no. 8) with its own little garden, but with just 14 rooms you'll need to book well in advance. Pet-friendly. *207 Darling-hurst Rd.* ☎ *02/9360 6000. www. altamont.com.au. 14 rooms. Doubles $130–$225. AE, DC, MC, V. Train: Kings Cross. Map p 134.*

**The Hughenden** WOOLLAHRA Boutique hotel in an 1870s mansion in the leafy eastern suburbs shopping and art gallery precinct. Close to the sports stadium and pet-friendly. *14 Queen St.* ☎ *02/9363 4863. www.thehughenden.com.au. 40 rooms. Doubles $178–$348. AE, DC, MC, V. Bus: 389. Map p 133.*

**★★★ InterContinental Sydney** CITY CENTRAL Behind the sandstone facade of the 1851 Treasury Building is an elegant five-star hotel overlooking the harbor and Opera House. Some rooms can be on the small side, but they do some interesting packages that way go beyond the usual tourist expectations. *117 Macquarie St. (corner Bridge & Phillip sts.).* ☎ *02/9253 9000. www.sydney. intercontinental.com.au. 509 rooms. Doubles $360–$525. AE, DC, MC, V. Train: Circular Quay. Map p 134.*

★★★ kids **Lane Cove River Tourist Park** LANE COVE   Get back to nature in Lane Cove National Park (p 81). Pitch a tent or opt for one of the pre-erected tents, park the camper van, or glamp it up in a luxury hard-floored safari tent complete with en-suite bathroom and wraparound deck. The two-bed-room cabins are a phenomenal value, especially if you're traveling with kids. *Plassey Rd., North Ryde.* ☎ *02/9888 9133. www.lanecove rivertouristpark.com.au. 28 cabins, 300 caravan & tent sites. Cabins $130–$150. Caravan/tent sites $35–$37. Tandara eco-tent $390–$450. MC, V. Bus: 545 from Chatswood Station. Map p 134.*

**The Macleay Hotel** POTTS POINT   A room with a view of the Opera House and Harbour Bridge for around $175 is about as good a deal as you'll ever find in Sydney, so snap it up. If none of those are available, the rooms on the east side have a fantastic water view over Elizabeth Bay. Rooms on the south side don't have district views, as promised, but a view of another building. *28 Macleay St.* ☎ *02/9357 7755. www. themacleay.com. 126 rooms. Doubles $175–$270. AE, DC, MC, V. Train: Kings Cross. Map p 134.*

★ **Marque Sydney** CITY CENTRAL   Freshly made over, this hotel offers good value if you want to be close to Central train station, or the Enter-tainment or Convention centers. Opt for an "executive" room, they're much quieter. *Corner George & Quay sts.* ☎ *02/9212 2544. www. marquehotels.com/sydney. 113*

rooms. Doubles $170–$230. AE, DC, MC, V. Train: Central. Map p 134.*

kids **Mercure Sydney** CITY CENTRAL   Smallish functional rooms, close to trains, Darling Har-bour, and the Convention Center. *818–820 George St.* ☎ *1800 633 948 or 02/9217 6666. www.mercure sydney.com.au. 517 rooms. Doubles $224–$314. AE, DC, MC, V. Train: Central. Map p 134.*

★ **Mercure Sydney Potts Point** KINGS CROSS   Great loca-tion in the heart of Kings Cross with newly refurbished rooms offering good value and knockout harbor views. *Corner Victoria St. & Darling-hurst Rd.* ☎ *02/9397 1777. www. mercure.com. 227 rooms. Doubles $179–$319. AE, DC, MC, V. Train: Kings Cross. Map p 134.*

kids **Novotel Sydney on Dar-ling Harbour** DARLING HAR-BOUR   Reasonably sized rooms great for business and convention travelers, which means you can often snare a good weekend deal. They have some great specials for kids. *100 Murray St.* ☎ *02/9934 0000. www.novoteldarlingharbour. com.au. 525 rooms. Doubles $305–$350. AE, DC, MC, V. Light rail/mono-rail: Convention. Map p 134.*

★★★ kids **The Observatory Hotel** THE ROCKS   Clubby, opulent, grand, and genteel; it's one of the city's most expensive hotels, but if you feel like being spoiled this is the place to stay. Check the website for package deals. Eat in at the excellent Galileo Restaurant and do some laps in the pool under the star-studded ceiling. Kids can adopt a goldfish to keep in their room. *89–113 Kent St.* ☎ *02/9256 2222. www.observatory hotel.com.au. 99 rooms. Doubles $445–$555. AE, DC, MC, V. Train: Cir-cular Quay. Map p 134.*

**★★★ Park Hyatt Sydney** THE ROCKS On the water, in the shadow of the Harbour Bridge and directly opposite the Opera House, this place has balcony rooms with the best views in town. It's one of the most expensive hotels in town, but perfect for that special occasion. *7 Hickson Rd.* ☎ *02/9241 1234. www. sydney.park.hyatt.com. 158 rooms. Doubles $855–$1,260. AE, DC, MC, V. Train: Circular Quay. Map p 134.*

**★ Q Station** MANLY There are great harbor views and plenty of atmosphere in the made-over first- and second-class quarters at the old Quarantine Station on North Head. Not all rooms have en-suite bathrooms, so check when booking. Best views are in the second-class section. *North Head Scenic Dr.* ☎ *02/9976 6220. www.qstation. com.au. 75 rooms. Doubles $260– $380. AE, DC, MC, V. Ferry: Manly. Bus: 135 from Manly Wharf. Map p 134.*

**Quay West Suites** THE ROCKS Sleek apartment hotel with drop-dead gorgeous city and harbor views. Great for mixing work and pleasure. *98 Gloucester St.* ☎ *02/ 9240 6000. www.mirvachotels.com/ quay-west-suites-sydney. 115 rooms. Doubles $287–$527. AE, DC, MC, V. Train: Circular Quay. Map p 134.*

**★★ Ravesi's** BONDI Brilliant beachside location in the center of Bondi. Upstairs rooms open out to great ocean views, downstairs is one of the most popular bars in Bondi, so pack earplugs if you want an early night. *Corner Campbell Parade & Hall St.* ☎ *02/9365 4422. www.ravesis.com.au. 12 rooms. Doubles $299–$499. AE, MC, V. Bus: 380. Map p 133.*

**The Russell Hotel** THE ROCKS Small boutique hotel in a charming building dating back to 1887. Rooms can be a bit chintzy and some have shared bathrooms, but it's a good value given the location. Check out the view from the rooftop garden. *143a George St.* ☎ *02/9241 3543. www.therussell.com.au. 29 rooms. Doubles $159–$299 w/breakfast. AE, DC, MC, V. Train: Circular Quay. Map p 134.*

*The luxe Observatory Hotel.*

*Embrace the elegance at the Shangri-La Hotel.*

### ★★★ Shangri-La Hotel THE
ROCKS Size matters—these are some of the largest rooms in the city with the best harbor views in town. *176 Cumberland St.* ☎ *02/9250 6000. www.shangri-la.com. 563 rooms. Doubles $395–$530. AE, DC, MC, V. Train: Circular Quay. Map p 134.*

### Sofitel Sydney Wentworth
CITY CENTER Brush shoulders with visiting celebrities and heads of state in this luxury five-star hotel. *61–101 Phillip St.* ☎ *1800 676 960 or 02/9230 0700. http://www.sofitel sydney.com.au/sydney.html. 436 rooms. Doubles $315–$465. AE, DC, MC, V. Train: Martin Place. Map p 134.*

### Swiss-Grand Resort & Spa
BONDI It's a bit of an eyesore from the outside, but who cares once you're inside enjoying your own ocean view. Don't bother if you can't get a room with a view, and check out the packages rather than the room-only rates. *Corner Campbell Parade & Beach Rd.* ☎ *1800 655 252 or 02/9365 5666. www.swiss grand.com.au. 203 rooms. Doubles $367–$432. AE, DC, MC, V. Bus: 378, 380. Map p 133.*

### ★★ kids Swissôtel Sydney CITY
CENTER Bright and cheery, this hotel suits both business travelers and families. Book a Swissôtel Kids Room and you'll get a room full of toys and passes to a range of family attractions. *68 Market St.* ☎ *02/9238 8888. www.swissotel.com. 359 rooms. Doubles $279–$349. AE, DC, MC, V. Train: Town Hall. Map p 134.*

### Sydney Central YHA CENTRAL
It's a backpackers' hostel with lots of dorm rooms but you can also get double rooms with en-suites. There's a great swimming pool, and it's right across the road from Central Station, so it's handy to just about everything. *Corner Pitt St. & Rawson Place.* ☎ *02/9218 9000. www.yha.com.au. 151 rooms. Doubles $100–$120. MC, V. Train: Central. Map p 134.*

★★★ **Sydney Harbour Marriott** CIRCULAR QUAY   Most rooms in this upmarket hotel have good harbor or Opera House views. Beds are supercomfortable, and you can usually get good packages online. *30 Pitt St.* ☎ *1800 302 738 or 02/9259 7000. www.marriott.com.au. 550 rooms. Doubles $339–$529. AE, DC, MC, V. Train: Circular Quay. Map p 134.*

★★★ **Sydney Harbour YHA** THE ROCKS   The only backpackers' accommodations in The Rocks, this new hostel has knockout harbor and Opera House views from the rooftop sun deck, as well as double rooms for around $150, which is about as cheap as a harbor view gets in Sydney. *110 Cumberland St.* ☎ *02/8272 0900. www.yha.com.au. 106 beds, 46 rooms with en-suites. Dorm beds $41. Doubles $145. MC, V. Train: Circular Quay. Map p 134.*

★ kids **Travelodge Sydney** CITY CENTER   Rooms are basic and plain, but are a good value in the heart of the city. *27 Wentworth Ave.* ☎ *02/8267 1700. www.travelodge.com.au. 406 rooms. Doubles $125–$230. AE, DC, MC, V. Train: Martin Place. Map p 134.*

★★★ **Vibe Hotel North Sydney** MILSONS POINT   Staying on the north shore of the city makes for a nice change, and it's a lovely stroll over the Harbour Bridge to get home. Ask for a Kirribilli view. *88 Alfred St.* ☎ *02/9955 1111. www.vibehotels.com.au. 165 rooms. Doubles $199–$399. AE, DC, MC, V. Train: Milsons Point. Map p 134.*

★★★ **Vibe Hotel Rushcutters** RUSHCUTTERS BAY   A quieter alternative to staying in town. The hotel fronts a lovely park on a small harbor bay and is just minutes from Kings Cross, Paddington, and Bondi. *100 Bayswater Rd.* ☎ *02/8353 8988. www.vibehotels.com.au. 245 rooms. Doubles $160–$355. AE, DC, MC, V. Train: Edgecliff. Map p 134.*

★★★ **Vibe Hotel Sydney** CITY CENTRAL   Vibe hotels always offer great value with a stylish colorful

*Backpackers and budgeters at the Sydney Harbour YHA.*

*A BLUE Sydney superior rafter room.*

edge. This one is very handy to both Central Station and the theater district. *111 Goulburn St.* ☎ *02/8272 3300. www.vibehotels.com.au. 190 rooms. Doubles $220–$280. AE, DC, MC, V. Train: Central. Map p 134.*

**The Westin Sydney** CITY CENTER   Luxury hotel in the former GPO building. The heritage rooms are in the historic section; the more contemporary tower rooms have great views (particularly from the bathrooms), and the workout rooms are equipped with private gym equipment. *1 Martin Place.* ☎ *02/ 8223 1111. www.westin.com.au/ sydney. 416 rooms. Doubles $460– $570. AE, DC, MC, V. Train: Martin Place. Map p 134.* ●

## Tips on Accommodations

Australia offers a wide range of accommodations to fit your budget and taste. It's a rare **hotel room** that does not have air-conditioning, a phone, color TV, clock radio, minifridge (or minibar), and self-serve coffee and tea. Private bathrooms are standard, but often are shower-only, no tub. A fully furnished **serviced apartment** with two bedrooms, living room, kitchen, laundry, and often two bathrooms starts around A$170 a night. Australia's plentiful **motels** are neat and clean, if often a little dated. Some have restaurants attached, and many have swimming pools. Rates average A$80 to A$120 double. **Bed & breakfasts** are cheap, plentiful, and easy to find for under A$100 for a double. Bathroom facilities may be shared at a B&B. Some Aussie **pubs** offer rooms, usually with shared bathrooms. It can be noisy, but rates are sometimes as low as A$50 per person a night. The Aussie answer to the dude ranch is a **farmstay.** Rooms can be anything from a basic bunkhouse to rustically luxurious digs. Many farms charge under A$200 for a double, which may include breakfast.

# The Blue Mountains

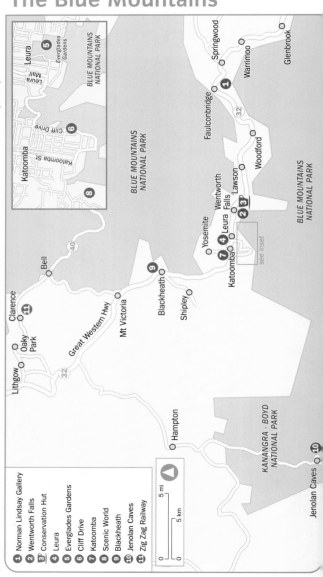

1. Norman Lindsay Gallery
2. Wentworth Falls
3. Conservation Hut
4. Leura
5. Everglades Gardens
6. Cliff Drive
7. Katoomba
8. Scenic World
9. Blackheath
10. Jenolan Caves
11. Zig Zag Railway

*Previous page: The Zig Zag Railway.*

The massive ridge of mountainous wilderness known as the Blue Mountains is around 90 minutes by car or train from the center of Sydney. Impenetrable for the first 25 years of the colony, the mountains were finally crossed in 1813 by the trio of Blaxland, Wentworth, and Lawson, finally opening up the western hinterland to settlement. It's an area of dramatic World Heritage–listed mountain scenery and is a great place to do some bushwalking or curl up in front of an open fire in winter, when snowfalls are not uncommon. There are lots of art galleries, historic houses, wonderful gardens, and many delightful coffee shops specializing in homemade scones and Devonshire teas. Is it any wonder it's a favorite for Sydneysiders and visitors alike?

**① ★★★ Norman Lindsay Gallery.** The former home of renowned Australian artist and author Norman Lindsay houses a collection of his oil paintings, watercolors, etchings, drawings, novels, sculpture, ship models, and memorabilia, set in extensive gardens. *⊕ 45 min. 12–14 Norman Lindsay Crescent, Faulconbridge. ☎ 02/4751 1067. www.normanlindsay.com.au. Admission $12 adults, $6 kids. Daily 10am–4pm.*

**② ★★★ Wentworth Falls.** Visit the Falls Gallery and walk along Falls Road from the Falls Reserve picnic area to Valley of the Waters, where a spectacular network of lookouts along the walking tracks offers dramatic views of cliff-top escarpments, waterfalls, and the Jamison Valley below. *⊕ 1 hr. Falls Gallery: 161 Falls Rd. ☎ 02/4757 1139. Wed–Sun & public holidays 10am–5pm.*

The **③ ★★★ kids Conservation Hut** is a great spot for lunch by the open fire with views over the edge of the escarpment. *Fletcher St., Wentworth Falls. ☎ 02/4757 3827. $$.*

**④ ★★★ Leura.** Known as the Garden Village, Leura has an annual Gardens Festival in October. It's also popular among shoppers—the main street, Leura Mall, is lined with art and craft galleries. *⊕ 1 hr.*

*Enjoying a tranquil moment in the Blue Mountains.*

# Getting There

You can catch a train to Katoomba from Central Station ($7.80 one-way adults, $3.90 kids), but to explore the best of the Blue Mountains a car is the best option. Alternatively, there are a range of tour companies that offer day bus trips to the area from Sydney. Another good option is the **Blue Mountains Explorer Bus** (☎ 1300 300 915; www.explorerbus.com.au) that allows you to hop on and hop off at 30 stops around Leura and Katoomba. It operates on a half-hourly basis from Katoomba Railway Station; the cost is $36 adults, $18 kids.

**⑤ ★★ Everglades Gardens.**
This National Trust garden created by Paul Sorenson in the 1930s is a magnificent cold-climate arboretum complete with formal terraces, Jamison Valley views, art and photo galleries, and refreshments in the Art Deco heritage residence. ⏱ *30 min. 37 Everglades Ave., Leura.*

*The awesome beauty of the Blue Mountains.*

☎ *02/4784 1938. Admission $8 adults, $4 kids. Daily 10am–5pm spring and summer, 10am–4pm autumn and winter.*

**⑥ ★★★ Cliff Drive.** Winding its way along the cliff's edge from Leura to Katoomba, this is a must-do if you have your own transport. Highlights include Leura Cascades, intriguing formations such as Mount Solitary, the Ruined Castle, Katoomba Falls and Cascades, and of course the Three Sisters at Echo Point in Katoomba. Be prepared to make lots of stops to photograph the amazing views. ⏱ *30 min.*

**⑦ ★★★ Katoomba.** Home to one of the most photographed spots in the state: the Three Sisters. The best view is from Echo Point, which is also the starting point of numerous bushwalks, including the Giant Stairway, one of the most popular short walks in the mountains. The track, which takes around 3 hours to complete, descends some 900-odd steps into the valley and along the base of the cliffs, and you can head back up aboard the Scenic Railway or take a ride on the Scenic Skyway or Cableway. ⏱ *30 min.*

**⑧ ★★★ kids Scenic World.**
Incorporating the Scenic Skyway, a 720m (2,362-ft.) cable-car ride, 270m

(886 ft.) above the valley floor, which you can see through the glass floor; the Scenic Railway, the steepest incline railway in the world; and the Scenic Cableway, a 545m (1,788-ft.) ride into, or out of, the World Heritage–listed rainforest of the Jamison Valley. ⏱ *30 min. Corner Violet St. & Cliff Dr., Katoomba.* ☎ *02/4780 0200. www.scenicworld.com.au. Admission Scenic Pass includes rides on all 3 attractions $28 adults, $14 kids. Daily 9am–5pm.*

**9** ★★ **Blackheath.** Check out Evans Lookout, the Bacchante Gardens, Pulpit Rock, or escape into the Grose Valley for a full day's walk. ⏱ *45 min.*

**10** ★★★ **kids Jenolan Caves.** There are 280 known caves in the Jenolan Reserve, many richly decorated with stunning limestone formations—stalactites and stalagmites, columns, shawls, and canopies. Eleven of the caves are open to the public and tours leave regularly. There are also candlelight ghost tours, "off the track" tours (where guides take you to their favorite secret places), and adventure caving tours. ⏱ *2 hr.* ☎ *1300 763 311 or 02/6359 3911. www. jenolancaves.org.au. There are no public transport facilities to Jenolan Caves, although many bus companies include it on their itineraries. Tour prices vary. Daily.*

**11** ★★★ **kids Zig Zag Railway.** If you're a history buff, a train enthusiast, or have kids in tow, a ride on the Zig Zag Railway at Clarence is a must. The railway was built between 1866 and 1869 and features a series of sloping tracks forming the letter Z with reversing stations at the top and bottom. The train is pulled by a steam locomotive. ⏱ *90 min. Clarence Railway Station, Clarence.* ☎ *02/6351 4826. www.zigzag railway.com.au. Admission adults $19 one-way, $30 return; kids $12 and $15. Trains leave Clarence daily 11am, 1pm, & 3pm.*

*The Three Sisters in Katoomba.*

# The Hunter Valley

The Best Day Trips & Excursions

1. Wollombi
2. Broke
3. Yengo National Park
4. Wine Country Visitors' Information Centre
5. Petersons Champagne House
6. Mistletoe Wines
7. Wyndham Estate
8. Hunter Valley Cheese Company
9. Hunter Valley Gardens
10. Hot-Air Ballooning
11. Hunter Valley Golf and Country Club
12. Cypress Lakes Golf and Country Club
13. The Vintage

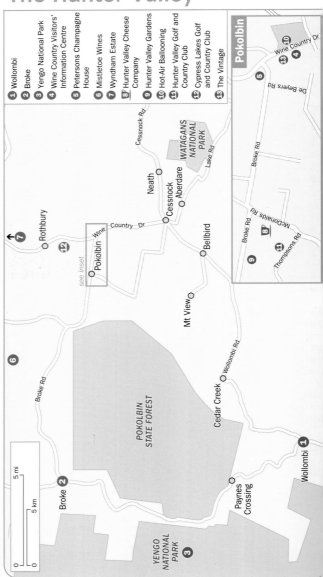

The Hunter Valley is home to some of Australia's best wineries and winemakers, as well as good restaurants, gardens, golf, and galleries. Just 2 hour's drive northwest of Sydney, the valleys and hills hide some wonderful historic villages that time seems to have sidestepped.

*The Wollombi General Store.*

**① ★★ Wollombi.** This tiny village, 30km (19 miles) southwest of Cessnock, is home to several antiques and gift stores. In the early 19th century the village was established on the Great North Road, a convict-built feat of road engineering that is still visible today. The Endeavour Museum in the old courthouse (c. 1866) has a collection of local history and is well worth the $2 entry fee (kids free). Pop into the Wollombi Tavern for a taste of the infamous Dr. Jurd's Jungle Juice. It's an acquired taste, but sipping a cold drink on the veranda overlooking the creek at the back of the hotel is a nice way to spend a few lazy hours. ⏱ *30 min. Endeavour Museum: Corner Wollombi & Maitland roads.* ☎ *02/ 4990 1788. Sat–Sun 10am–4pm.*

## Getting There

If you're driving from Sydney, the best way to get to the Hunter is to take the F3 north to the Cessnock exit. This is the main vineyard area and you can pick up lots of information from the visitor center on the outskirts of town. Head out to Pokolbin, Broke, and Lovedale and follow the signs to whichever winery takes your fancy. But if you're not in a hurry, take the scenic back road north from the Central Coast through Bucketty and Wollombi.

# Wine Tasting

With more than 120 wineries and cellar doors in the area, you won't get to see them all for ★★★ **wine tasting,** but most are open daily 10am to 5pm. I've listed just a few of my favorites, but call into any that take your fancy. The area is most famous for its Semillon and Shiraz (Syrah) wines.

*Wollombi Tavern: Old North Rd., Wollombi.* ☎ *02/4998 3261.*

**2 Continue on to Broke.** It skirts the Broken Back Range, and you'll start to see more vines and less cattle. If you've got a four-wheel-drive, explore the steep gorges and rocky ridges of Yengo National Park (see below). ⏱ *30 min.*

**3 Yengo National Park.** Part of the Greater Blue Mountains World Heritage area, the northern section, near Broke, is one of the state's least visited national parks and has some great Aboriginal rock carvings. ⏱ *2 hr.*

**4 Wine Country Visitors' Information Center.** Pick up a free winery map. ⏱ *15 min.* 455

*Wine Country Dr., Pokolbin.* ☎ *02/ 4990 0900. www.winecountry.com. au. Daily 9am–5pm.*

**5 Petersons Champagne House.** Great bubbly. *Corner Broke Rd. & Wine Country Dr., Pokolbin.* ☎ *02/4998 7881. Daily 9am–5pm.*

**6 Mistletoe Wines.** Home to the Pokolbin Gallery and Mistletoe Sculpture Garden and a great, easy-drinking rosé. *771 Hermitage Rd., Pokolbin.* ☎ *1800 055 080 or 02/4998 7770. Daily 10am–6pm.*

**7 Wyndham Estate.** One of Australia's oldest wineries and the birthplace of Australian Shiraz. *700 Dalwood Rd., Dalwood.* ☎ *02/4938 3444. Daily 9:30am–4:30pm.*

*Hunter Valley Gardens, the Brokenback Brummies.*

Watch cheese being made and go on a cheese-making tour at  **8** ★★★ **Hunter Valley Cheese Company.** Or simply browse the well stocked produce room for just about anything you need to build a picnic (many of the vineyards have great picnic areas) with local olive oils, jams, mustards, spreads, pâtés, dried fruits, breads, and of course cheese. Their signature cheese—the washed rind—is superb. *McDonalds Rd., Pokolbin.* ☎ *02/4998 7744. $.*

**9** ★★★ kids **Hunter Valley Gardens.** There are 8km (5 miles) of pathways to wander among the 12 themed gardens, including a story-book garden for the kids. More than 6,000 trees, 600,000 shrubs, and 1,000,000 ground covers have transformed the site into one of the most impressive gardens in the country. A cafeteria and gift shop are on-site and next door is the Hunter Gardens Village with 15 boutique and specialty stores. ⏱ *90 min. Broke Rd., Pokolbin.* ☎ *02/4998 4000. www. hvg.com.au. Admission $24 adults, $12 kids, $54 family. Daily 9am–5pm.*

**10** ★★★ **Hot-Air Ballooning.** Like many of Australia's popular wine-growing and weekend getaway areas, the Hunter is a popular place to go hot-air ballooning and several operators offer dawn flights over the valley. Almost all include champagne breakfasts and round-trip transport. Flights depart from Cessnock Airport approximately 1 hour before dawn. ⏱ *3–4 hr. Cessnock Airport, Wine*

*Hot air ballooning the Hunter.*

*Country Dr., Pokolbin.* ☎ *02/4990 0900. www.winecountry.com.au. Admission $299–$335 adults, $235 kids.*

**11** **Hunter Valley Golf and Country Club.** *Corner Allandale & Lovedale roads, Pokolbin.* ☎ *02/ 4991 4777. 18 holes $59–$69.*

**12** **Cypress Lakes Golf & Country Club.** The Golden Door Spa is on the resort's grounds, for those partners who prefer massages and pampering to hacking and chipping. *Corner McDonalds & Thompsons roads, Pokolbin.* ☎ *02/ 4993 1555. 18 holes $65–$110.*

**13** **The Vintage.** Ranks as one of the country's best courses; owned by Greg Norman. *Vintage Dr., Rothbury.* ☎ *02/4998 2208. www.thevintage. com.au. 18 holes $104–$129.*

## Golf

If you like golf then you'll love **golfing the Hunter.** There are ★★★ three premium courses in the valley.

# The Grand Pacific Drive

1. Royal National Park
2. Stanwell Tops
3. Symbio Wildlife Gardens
4. Lawrence Hargrave Drive and Sea Cliff Bridge
5. Chedo's Café
6. Wollongong
7. Nan Tien Buddhist Temple
8. Australia's Industry World
9. Kiama blowhole and lighthouse
10. Jamberoo Action Park
11. Minnamurra Rainforest in Budderoo National Park
12. Illawarra Fly

he Grand Pacific Drive runs along a man-made cliff-hugging ledge between the pounding surf and towering escarpment wall north of Wollongong. The road is named after the aeronautical pioneer Lawrence Hargrave who made aviation history by rising 5m (16 ft.) above the ground strapped to a huge box kite in 1894 at Stanwell Park.

### ❶ ★★ Royal National Park.

The trip begins just south of the city in the world's second-oldest national park, where Lady Wakehurst Drive winds through eucalyptus forests, over windswept heathlands, and across low-level river weirs. Tracks spear off to beaches and lookouts and there are dozens of great picnic and swimming spots along the way. So close to Sydney, it's a popular place on sunny weekends—traffic snarls can be frustrating—but if you can time your drive for a weekday, you'll pretty much have the park to yourself. ⏱ *1 hr. www.nationalparks.nsw. gov.au. Admission $11 per vehicle. See p 81.*

### ❷ ★★★ Stanwell Tops.

Leaving Royal National Park, the road bursts out of the bush at Stanwell Tops, the cliff-top vantage point where paragliders and hang-gliders soar the thermals rising from the ocean below, emulating Australia's pioneer of flight, Lawrence Hargrave. On a clear day, you can see as far south as Wollongong. ⏱ *10 min.*

### ❸ ★★ kids Symbio Wildlife Gardens.

Unpack a picnic or fire up a barbecue, check out the crocodiles,

*Parasailing high above Stanwell Tops.*

koalas, meerkats, or any of the other 1,000 animals in the park, and cool off in the swimming pool at this down-to-earth zoo. ⏱ *2 hr. Lawrence Hargrave Dr., Helensburgh. ☎ 02/ 4294 1244. www.symbiozoo.com.au. Admission $24 adults, $15 kids. Daily 9:30am–5pm.*

## Getting There

You'll need a car to get the best out of this day trip. From the center of Sydney, head south past the airport, following the signs to Wollongong. Near Sutherland, you'll start to see the first of the Grand Pacific Drive signs, so leave the highway and head south through the Royal National Park and onto Lawrence Hargrave Drive.

*Sea Cliff Bridge.*

**4 ★★★ Lawrence Hargrave Drive & Sea Cliff Bridge.** Originally built to service the coal mines that have been hollowed out of the escarpment like Swiss cheese, the road was literally carved into the claystone and sandstone. Trouble was, these cliffs kept crumbling into the sea, often taking sections of the road with them. After dozens of near misses, the road was finally closed in 2003 while a solution was formulated: a 665m-long (2,181-ft.) multispan balanced cantilever bridge that curves around the cliffs 50m (164 ft.) out to sea, out of the way of any rockfalls. ⏱ *30 min.*

Good value pastas and Mediterranean platters make **5 ★★ Chedo's Café** a great spot for lunch. *748 Lawrence Hargrave Dr., Coledale.* ☎ *02/4268 3000. $–$$.*

**6 ★★★ Wollongong.** The third-largest city in NSW and a major coal, iron, and steel producing region, Wollongong is also one of the most attractive seaside cities in the country. Explore the horseshoe-shaped cove of Wollongong Harbour with its lighthouse, fishing fleet, fish markets, and wonderful city beaches. ⏱ *2 hr.*

**7 ★★ Nan Tien Buddhist Temple.** The largest Buddhist temple in the Southern Hemisphere offers a fascinating insight into modern Buddhism with classes in Tai Chi, meditation, calligraphy, and the indispensable skill of lotus-flower folding. ⏱ *45 min. Berkeley Rd., Berkeley.* ☎ *02/4272 0600. www. nantien.org.au. Free admission. Tues–Sun 9am–5pm.*

**8 Australia's Industry World.** Take a guided tour of the massive Port Kembla Steelworks that was once the economic backbone of the city. ⏱ *2½ hr. Springhill Rd., Coniston.* ☎ *02/4275 7023. www.aiw.org. au. Admission $18 adults, $14 kids (minimum age 10). Tours Wed & Fri 9:30am–noon and you must wear flat enclosed shoes and long trousers. Bookings essential.*

**9 ★★★ Kiama Blowhole and Lighthouse.** A sea-cliff cave that periodically blows water as high as 60m (197 ft.) in the air, most spectacularly when the wind and water are coming from the southeast. **Caution:** Stand back! It is floodlit until 9:30pm. The 1887 lighthouse is nearby. ⏱ *15 min. Blowhole Point, Kiama.*

**10** ★★★ **kids** **Jamberoo Action Park.** A massive water park with a new wave pool/man-made beach, water slides, thrill rides, chair lifts, and toboggan rides. There are pools designed for all ages, from toddlers to teenagers. ⏱ *2–4 hr. Jamberoo Rd., Jamberoo.* ☎ *02/4236 0114. Admission $39 adults & kids 13 and over, $31 kids 4–12, free for kids 3 and under. Daily 10am–5pm, Sept to end of Apr.*

**11** ★★★ **kids** **Minnamurra Rainforest.** A boardwalk leads from the Minnamurra Rainforest Centre through subtropical and temperate rainforest areas to Minnamurra Falls. *In the Budderoo National Park.* ⏱ *2 hr. Minnamurra Falls Rd., near Jamberoo.* ☎ *02/4236 0469. Admission $11 per vehicle. Daily 9am–5pm.*

**12** ★★ **kids** **Illawarra Fly.** A 500m-long (1,640-ft.), 25m-high (82-ft.) elevated tree-top walk. For

*Jamberoo Action Park.*

those with a head for heights there's a 45m-high (148-ft.) lookout, while thrill-seekers can take a bounce on the edge of the springboard cantilevers. ⏱ *45 min. 182 Knights Hill Rd., Knights Hill.* ☎ *02/4885 1010. www.illawarrafly. com. Admission $24 adults, $10 kids. Daily 9am–5pm.*

*Illawara treetop walk.*

# Central Coast

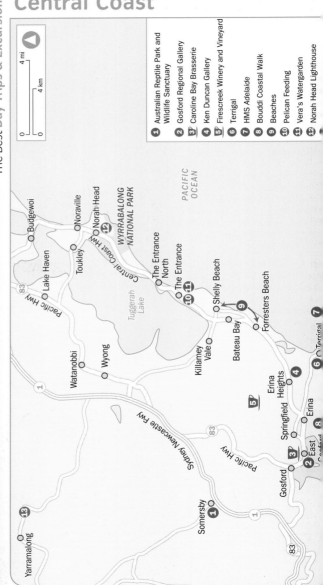

1 Australian Reptile Park and Wildlife Sanctuary
2 Gosford Regional Gallery
3 Caroline Bay Brasserie
4 Ken Duncan Gallery
5 Firescreek Winery and Vineyard
6 Terrigal
7 HMS Adelaide
8 Bouddi Coastal Walk
9 Beaches
10 Pelican Feeding
11 Vera's Watergarden
12 Norah Head Lighthouse

The area of beachside villages and towns known collectively as the Central Coast is 2 hours north of the city, making it a favorite weekend destination for Sydneysiders. The Central Coast offers great surfing beaches and national parks with stunning lookouts and lots of kid-friendly attractions.

**1** ★★★ **kids** **Australian Reptile Park and Wildlife Sanctuary.** More than just a zoo, this wildlife park is the sole Australian provider of venom which is used for snake and funnel-web spider anti-venoms. It's one of the only places in the country you can watch the snakes being milked of their deadly poison. Children love meeting the platypus, kangaroos, and wombats and having their photograph taken with a huge python or one of the koalas. Spiderworld and the Lost World of Reptiles are fun theme-park-type exhibits with lots of interactive activities for the kids. 🕐 *2 hr.* *Pacific Hwy., Somersby.* ☎ *02/4340 1146. www.reptilepark.com.au. Admission $26 adults, $14 kids. Daily 9am–5pm.*

**2** ★★ **Gosford Regional Gallery.** Three gallery spaces show contemporary and traditional art by Australian artists. Exhibits change regularly, and the gallery is also

*The Gosford Regional Gallery's Edogawa Japanese Gardens.*

home to the Edogawa Japanese Gardens, one of the best examples of a traditional Japanese garden in regional Australia. The gift shop is a great place to find affordable, locally made, hand-crafted pieces. 🕐 *30*

*Australian Reptile Park.*

The Best Day Trips & Excursions

*Enjoy fruity wine at Firescreek.*

min. 36 Webb St., East Gosford. ☎ 02/4325 0056. www.gosford regionalgallery.com. Free admission. Gallery daily 10am–4pm. Gardens daily 9:30am–4:30pm.

Relax over a glass of wine at lunchtime inside the art gallery at ③ **Caroline Bay Brasserie,** looking out over the peaceful gardens. *36 Webb St., East Gosford.* ☎ *02/ 4324 8099. $–$$.*

④ ★ **Ken Duncan Gallery.** Changing display of panoramic Australian landscape photographs.

*Ruins of the HMAS Adelaide.*

🕐 *15 min. 414 The Entrance Rd., Erina Heights.* ☎ *02/4367 6701. Free admission. Daily 10am–5pm.*

⑤ **Firescreek Winery and Vineyard.** Try a glass of Pink Fig Wine or Parsley & Lime at this tiny little winery that makes wine from just about anything you can think of—except grapes. My favorite is the sweet and sticky Apricot Ambrosia, which goes perfectly with a slice of rich double chocolate mud cake. Yum! 🕐 *30 min. 192 Wattle Tree Rd., Holgate.* ☎ *02/ 4365 0768. www.firescreek.com.au. Free admission. Wine tasting 10am– 5pm Wed–Sun.*

⑥ **Terrigal.** A year-round seaside resort crowded with visitors and locals enjoying the cafes, restaurants, and boutiques selling everything from New Age crystals and antiques to swimwear and designer clothing. The spectacular Terrigal beach is opposite the main street, and the fish co-op beside the Skillion headland serves great fresh fish ready to eat on the beach. 🕐 *1 hr. Terrigal Esplanade, Terrigal.*

⑦ **Dive HMAS Adelaide.** In April 2011 the HMAS *Adelaide* was scuttled off Avoca Beach, making it

Cool off at Vera's Water garden.

the first military dive site in NSW. The 138m-long (453-ft.) naval frigate, which served from 1980 until January 2008, rests on the seabed in around 32m (105 ft.) of water and is open to divers of all levels. Book a guided dive tour through local dive shops; details are available from Central Coast visitor centers. ⏱ 2 hr. ☎ 02/4343 4444. www.hmas adelaide.com. Dive permits $18. Tour prices vary. Daily 6am–6:30pm.

**8 ★★★ Bouddi Coastal Walk.** If you've got time, and can organize a pickup by car (or call a taxi) at one end, this is a terrific 4-hour walk in Bouddi National Park with fantastic views along the coast, including the distant Sydney skyline. Start the walk from the eastern end of Putty Beach and then head up to the lookout at Gerrin Point, where you might be lucky enough to see whales between May and November. The walk then hops from beach to beach before it ends at MacMasters Beach. Best place for a dip: Maitland Bay. ⏱ 4 hr.

**9 Beaches.** If you have come to the Central Coast for the beaches you won't be disappointed. Follow the Scenic Highway (which, despite its grand name, is more of a twisting country road) to Avoca and Copacabana, where you'll find long stretches of sand and surf. Continue north along The Entrance Road, passing yet more white sandy beaches, most usually more deserted than busy Terrigal or Avoca. Wamberal, Forresters, and Shelly Beach are all favorites with locals and surfers. **Warning:** The beaches are usually unpatrolled, so take care when swimming. ⏱ 2–3 hr.

**10 ★★ kids Pelican Feeding.** Every day at 3:30pm scores of squawking pelicans swarm the shores of Memorial Park for a daily feed of fish. It's free to watch and children love it. ⏱ 15 min. Memorial Park, The Entrance.

**11 ★★★ kids Vera's Water Garden.** A free play pool with lots of colorful sculptures to climb on in the heart of The Entrance makes

*The Norah Head light.*

great summer fun for kids. ⏲ *30 min. Memorial Park, The Entrance.*

⓬ ★★ **Norah Head Lighthouse.** From The Entrance, continue north on the narrow strip of land that separates Tuggerah Lake from the sea, through Wyrrabalong National Park to Noraville, and take the turnoff to Norah Head Lighthouse. Built in 1903, the lighthouse is open for tours on weekends, and the view is beautiful. A walking track skirts around the side of the lighthouse and leads to stairs that lead down to the rock platform below and to Lighthouse Beach, a popular fishing spot. ⏲ *30 min. Bush St., Norah Head.* ☎ *1300 132 975. Admission $10 adults, $6 kids. Sat–Sun 10am.*

⓭ ★ **Yarramalong Valley.** Drive inland to Wyong, along the lake shore and then into the lush green valley beside Wyong Creek to Yarramalong. This is a very scenic drive, past farmland, horse studs, orchards and grazing cattle. ⏲ *45 min.* ●

## Getting There

Though you can catch a train to Gosford from Central Station ($7.80 adults, $3.90 kids one-way), public transport is limited once you're there—making your own vehicle the best option.

# The
# Savvy Traveler

# Before You Go

## Government Tourist Offices

Destination NSW is the best source for information on Sydney and surrounding areas. Their website, www.visitnsw.com, has details on attractions, hotels, events, transport, and more. Tourism Australia (www.australia.com) is another good source of information.

**In the U.S.:** Tourism NSW, Suite 810, 8th floor, 6100 Center Dr., Los Angeles, CA 90045. ☎ 310/695-3235.

**In the U.K.:** Tourism NSW, Level 6, Australia Centre, Strand, London WC2B 4LG. ☎ 020/7438 4644.

**In New Zealand:** Tourism NSW, Level 3, 125 The Strand, Parnell, Auckland. ☎ 09/307 7040.

## The Best Time to Go

Sydney is blessed with a temperate climate and a range of year-round events, which means there is no bad time to visit. My favorite time to be in Sydney is January, when most of the locals are on holiday so traffic is lighter and the Sydney Festival is in full swing (see below).

## Festivals & Special Events

SUMMER. The city lights up for Christmas, and there's **Carols in the Domain** (www.carolsinthe domain.com), a free concert for those who like to sing. The **Sydney-Hobart Yacht Race** gets underway on Boxing Day (Dec 26) and the spectacle of 100 or more yachts under full sail as they leave the harbor is a pretty amazing sight. On **New Year's Eve** the city celebrates with a mega fireworks show—or two, to be exact. The main show is at 9pm so young kids and those who like their sleep don't miss out.

You'll need to get there early to secure the best harborside spots. The **Sydney Festival** is 3 weeks of nonstop theater, dance, music, and visual arts, as well as some fantastic free outdoor concerts (www.sydney festival.org.au). **Australia Day** celebrates the anniversary of the First Fleet's arrival at Sydney Cove on January 26 in 1788. It's celebrated across the country and is a public holiday, but nowhere puts on a bigger party than Sydney where it all began. A traditional Indigenous ceremony in the Royal Botanic Gardens marks the official start of the celebration, and it ends with a fireworks display once the sun goes down. Sydney's **Chinese New Year Festival** (late Jan to early Feb) is the largest Lunar New Year celebration outside Asia. Sydney becomes the center of the gay universe during the month-long **Sydney Gay & Lesbian Mardi Gras** festival that culminates in a parade of costumed dancers and decorated floats down Oxford Street (www.mardigras.org.au).

AUTUMN. Australia's largest annual event, the **Sydney Royal Easter Show** (www.eastershow.com.au) is 14 days of action-packed entertainment for all age groups, with animal pavilions and agricultural displays, carnival rides, and showbags galore. **Anzac Day,** April 25, is Australia's national day of mourning for those who died in wars and conflict. The city stops for a dawn service and street parade for returned servicemen and women. It's the one day of the year that two-up, a gambling game based around the tossing of three pennies, is legal and is played in pubs across the city in the

*Previous page: A span of the Sea Cliff Bridge bypasses the dangerous cliffs along Lawrence Hargrave Drive.*

# Useful Websites

www.visitnsw.com.au: where to go and what to see from Destination New South Wales

www.sydney.com: more information from Destination New South Wales, focusing just on Sydney and surrounds

www.sydneyairport.com.au: information about Sydney airport

www.131500.info: everything you need to plan your trip on Sydney's public transport system

www.mynrma.com.au: everything you need to know about motoring in NSW

www.whereis.com: online maps and driving directions

www.sydney.citysearch.com.au: for events, entertainment, dining, and shopping

www.yourrestaurants.com.au: restaurant and bar reviews

www.eatability.com.au/au/sydney: another good site with lots of restaurant reviews and tips and comments from diners

www.timeoutsydney.com.au: independent entertainment bible

afternoon. **Darling Harbour Hoopla** is Sydney's only acrobatic and street theater festival and runs across the Easter long weekend at different locations within Darling Harbour (www.darlingharbour.com). Bookworms are in heaven during the annual **Sydney Writers Festival** with a week-long festival of book readings, author talks, workshops and readings (www.swf. org.au).

WINTER. **Vivid Sydney** lights up Sydney with luminous art installations, including stunning light projections that paint the sails of the Opera House in a kaleidoscope of colors, or at least it has in years gone by—but who knows what will be in store next year? It's on mid-May to Mid-June (www.vividsydney. com). Catch a premiere at the **Sydney Film Festival** (http://www. sff.org.au), held over 19 days in June. Chill out at the **Darling Harbour Jazz Festival,** held over a long weekend, usually the first or second weekend in June (www.

darlingharbour.com). Held every 2 years (next one is in 2014), the **Biennale of Sydney** is a citywide festival of contemporary international art that runs June until early September (www.biennaleofsydney. com.au). Join 50,000 Sydneysiders on the 14km (8⅔-mile) **Sun-Herald City2Surf** "fun run" from the city to Bondi Beach in July. Runners take it pretty seriously, but plenty of people walk it or even push a stroller, and there's an inexplicably large number who do it in a gorilla suit (☎ 1800 555 514; www.city2surf. com.au).

SPRING. Fly a kite at the **Festival of the Winds,** Australia's largest and most exciting kite-flying festival held off Bondi Beach (www.waverley. nsw.gov.au). Dance it up at **Darling Harbour Fiesta,** the biggest Latin American and Spanish festival in Australia, held on the October long weekend, usually the first weekend of the month (www.darlingharbour. com). Don't miss **Sculpture by the Sea,** a 3-week outdoor exhibition of

| SYDNEY'S AVERAGE TEMPERATURE & RAINFALL | | | | | | |
|---|---|---|---|---|---|---|
| | JAN | FEB | MAR | APR | MAY | JUNE |
| Daily temp (°F) | 79 | 79 | 77 | 72 | 66 | 63 |
| Daily temp (°C) | 26 | 26 | 25 | 22 | 19 | 17 |
| Avg. Rainfall (in./mm) | 4/102 | 4.5/118 | 5/130 | 4.9/126 | 4.8/121 | 5.1/131 |
| | JULY | AUG | SEPT | OCT | NOV | DEC |
| Daily temp (°F) | 61 | 63 | 66 | 72 | 75 | 77 |
| Daily temp (°C) | 16 | 17 | 19 | 22 | 24 | 25 |
| Avg. Rainfall (in./mm) | 3.8/98 | 3.2/82 | 2.7/69 | 3/77 | 3.3/84 | 3/78 |

international sculptures lining the Bronte to Bondi cliff-top walk (www. sculpturebythesea.com).

## The Weather

Summer—November through to March—can be humid and sometimes quite rainy, while winter—June to August—can be quite cold at night. In winter most days are sunny and mild, although it's too cold for swimming at any of the beaches or outdoor pools. The few times a year the mercury drops into single digits will have locals moaning that they are freezing—quite amusing for those from colder climes.

## Cellphones (Mobiles)

Australia is on the GSM (Global System for Mobiles) network, so as long as your cellphone is called a mobile in Australia, is world-capable and you have activated global roaming (contact your service provider to check) you should be able to make and receive calls pretty much anywhere in Sydney, although reception is patchy once you leave the city. Not all North American phones are GSM, but you can rent one before leaving home from InTouch U.S.A. (☎ 800/872-7626; www. intouchglobal.com) or RoadPost

(☎ 888/290-1606 or 905/272-5665; www.roadpost.com). InTouch will also, for free, advise you on whether your existing phone will work overseas (☎ 703/222-7161, 9am–4pm EST, or go to www.intouchglobal. com/travel.htm). If you plan on making a lot of calls, consider buying a pay-as-you go phone in Sydney for more attractive call costs. There are outlets at all major airports and in most shopping centers.

## Car Rentals

Most of the major sights and attractions in Sydney are readily accessible by public transport. Parking in the city center can be problematic and expensive, so if you are just exploring the city don't bother with a hired car. If you are planning on doing some day trips or traveling further afield, however, a car is a good idea as public transport in most towns outside the city is pretty much nonexistent. All major car rental companies operate in Australia, and cars can be picked up at the airport and some hotels. The website www.vroom.com.au is a great place to compare costs across all major companies. **Remember:** Australians drive on the left.

# Getting **There**

### By Plane
Sydney International Airport is 8km (5 miles) from the city center. There are three terminals: T1 is the international terminal; T2 is home to a number of domestic and regional airlines, including Jetstar, Virgin Australia, Regional Express (REX), Aeropelican, AirLink, and Qantas (flights QF1600 and above); T3 is the terminal for domestic Qantas (flights QF0400–1599). **Taxis** from the airport to the city center cost \$35 to \$40, depending on traffic conditions. The **Airport Link** train connects the international and domestic airports to the city stations of Central, Museum, St. James, Circular Quay, Wynyard, and Town Hall. You'll need to change trains for other Sydney stations. Trains run approximately every 10 minutes, the journey into the city takes 15 minutes, and a one-way fare from T1 to Central costs \$16 adults, \$10 kids. It can get crowded during peak hour (approximately 7–9am and 4–6:30pm) and the trains do not have dedicated luggage racks. If you have lots of luggage and you're traveling into the city at these times, it's probably best to take an airport bus (see below) or a taxi. **Sydney Airporter** coaches (☎ 02/9666 9988; www.kst.com.au) operate to the city center from bus stops outside the terminals every 15 minutes. This service will drop you off at hotels in the city, Kings Cross, and Darling Harbour. Pickups from hotels require at least 3 hours' advance notice, and you get a discount if you book online the day before you travel. Tickets cost \$18 one-way and \$32 round-trip from the airport. The return portion can be used any time in the future.

### By Car
If you're driving you'll enter Sydney from the north on the Pacific Highway, from the south on the M5 and Princes Highway, and from the west on the Great Western Highway. All of the major freeways in and out of the city—including the Harbour Bridge, Harbour Tunnel, and Cross City Tunnel—have tolls, and most are not payable with cash. You can get an E-Toll pass before you travel or up to 48 hours after you traveled (☎ 13 18 65; www.rta.nsw.gov.au). Be mindful of T2 and T3 transit lanes; you must have two or three people in the car, respectively, in order to travel in these lanes.

### By Train
**Central Station** (☎ 13 15 00 for CityRail, or 13 22 32 for CountryLink interstate trains) is the main city and interstate train station. All interstate trains depart from here, and it's a major hub for suburban trains. Many city buses leave from neighboring Railway Square.

### By Bus
The **Sydney Coach Terminal** (☎ 02/9281 9366) is on the corner of Eddy Avenue and Pitt Street, next to Central Station. All major regional and interstate bus services arrive and depart from here.

### By Cruise Ship
Cruise ships dock at the **Overseas Passenger Terminal** in The Rocks (opposite the Sydney Opera House), or in Darling Harbour.

# Getting **Around**

## Discount Travel Passes

The **MyMulti Day Pass** allows unlimited bus, train, light rail, and ferry travel for 1 day. Tickets cost $20 for adults and $10 for kids. The pass is available at all bus, train, and ferry ticket outlets.

For $2.50 you get unlimited travel on all trains, buses, and ferries on Sunday with the **Family Fun Day Sunday** pass. To qualify for the discount the traveling group must be related and include at least one child and one adult.

A **Weekly Travel Pass** allows unlimited travel on buses, trains, and ferries. There are three different passes depending on the distance you need to travel. The pass visitors most commonly use is the **MyMulti1,** which covers all transportation within the city center and near surroundings ($41 adults, $21 kids). You can buy the pass at newsdealers or bus, train, and ferry ticket outlets.

## By Bus

**Buses** cover a wide area of metropolitan Sydney and are usually frequent and reliable. The minimum fare is $2 for adults and $1 for children for a 4km (2½-mile) "section," which covers most short hops in the city. Sections are marked on bus stops, but if in doubt, just tell the bus driver your destination and he'll work out the fare. More and more bus routes are being converted to prepay only, which means you can't buy your ticket on the bus. Tickets are available from newsdealers and convenience stores, CityRail train stations, and Sydney Ferries wharves.

**Free 555 Bus:** This free city shuttle operates every 10 minutes in both directions between 9:30am and 3:30pm on weekdays (until 9pm on Thurs nights) and between 9:30am and 6pm on weekends. It runs in a loop from Central down Elizabeth Street to Circular Quay and back up George Street to Chinatown and Central.

A **TravelTen** ticket offers 10 bus rides for a discounted price. A **MyBus1** TravelTen covers two sections on the bus route ($16 adults, $8 kids); a **MyBus2** TravelTen covers up to nine sections ($26 adults, $13 kids).

Most buses bound for the northern suburbs, including night buses to Manly and the bus to Taronga Zoo, leave from **Wynyard Park** on Carrington Street, behind the Wynyard Station on George Street. Buses to the southern beaches, such as Bondi and Bronte, and the western and eastern suburbs leave from **Circular Quay and Railway Square,** (George St., near Central Station).

For help planning your trip, call the **Transport Infoline** for information (☎ 13 15 00), visit www. 131500.info, or ask the staff at the bus information kiosk on the corner of Alfred and Loftus streets, behind Circular Quay Station.

## By Ferry

Ferries are a great way to get around Sydney. Almost all ferries leave from **Circular Quay.** For ferry information, call ☎ 13 15 00 or visit the ferry information office opposite Wharf 4. Timetables are available for all routes. One-way journeys within the inner harbor (virtually everywhere except Manly and Parramatta) cost $5.30 for adults and $2.60 for kids ages 4 to 15. Kids 3 and under travel free.

167

The ferry to Manly takes 30 minutes and leaves from Wharf 3 ($6.60 adults, $3.20 kids). Ferries run 6am to midnight.

If you plan on doing a lot of ferry travel, the TravelTen ferry ticket is good for 10 trips within the inner harbor, excluding Manly ($42 adults, $21 kids). Buy TravelTen tickets at newsdealers, bus depots, or the Circular Quay ferry terminal. TravelTen tickets are transferable, so if two or more people travel together, you can use the same ticket.

## By Train
Sydney's subway and train system is a quick way to get around, although timetable information should be used as a guide rather than gospel and it's not the safest option late at night, particularly if traveling to the outer suburbs. The main station is **Central Station,** although you can also pick up most trains at **Town Hall** and **Redfern** as well. One-way tickets within the city center cost $3.20 for adults and $1.60 for kids; return tickets are double that. Information is available from the Transport Infoline (☎ 13 15 00).

## By Light Rail & Monorail
The light rail system runs between **Central Station** and **Wentworth Park** in Pyrmont, providing good access to Chinatown, Paddy's Markets, Darling Harbour, the Star City casino, and the Sydney Fish Markets. They run every 10 minutes. One-way fares are $3.40 to $4.40 for adults and $2.20 to $3.40 for kids ages 4 to 15, depending on distance, and you can buy tickets from conductors on board. Seldom used by Sydneysiders, the monorail connects the CBD to Darling Harbour. The trip takes around 12 minutes vs. around 15 to walk it from Town Hall, which explains why it's not used by locals. Tickets are $4.90, free for

kids 4 and under (☎ 02/8584 5288; www.metrotransport.com.au).

## City Sightseeing Sydney & Bondi Explorer Buses
The bright red open-top **City Sightseeing** buses travel a 28km (17-mile) loop and stop at a number of places of interest, including the Sydney Opera House, the Royal Botanic Gardens, the State Library, Mrs. Macquaries Chair, the Art Gallery of New South Wales, Elizabeth Bay House, Sydney Tower, Chinatown, Darling Harbour, and The Rocks. The full circuit takes 90 minutes and you can hop on and off as often as you like. Buses depart from Circular Quay at 15- to 20-minute intervals. The blue **Bondi Explorer** also operates every day, traveling a 30km (19-mile) circuit around the eastern harborside bays and coastal beaches, including Watsons Bay, Bondi Beach, Bronte Beach, Coogee Beach, Paddington, Oxford Street, and Martin Place. The full circuit takes 90 minutes and you can hop on and off as often as you like, as well. The bus departs from Eddy Avenue opposite Central Station at 30- to 45-minute intervals.

Tickets for either bus cost $35 for adults, $20 for kids aged 4 to 16, and $80 for a family. Two-day tickets are $56 adults, $32 children, and $128 for a family. Buy tickets on the buses. Information is available at ☎ 02/9567 8400 or www.city-sight seeing.com/tour-Sydney.

## By Taxi
All taxi journeys are metered, although some trips attract a surcharge, including a trip across the Harbour Bridge or through the Harbour Tunnel and the Eastern Distributor from the airport, and all fares are 20% more expensive between 10pm and 6am. An extra 10% will be added to your fare if you pay by

credit card. Taxis line up at stands in the city, such as those opposite Circular Quay and Central Station. They are also frequently found in front of hotels. You can also hail a taxi in the street: a yellow light on top of the cab means it's vacant. Cabs can be hard to get on Friday and Saturday nights and around 3pm every day (when cabbies change shifts). Pas-

sengers must wear seatbelts in the front and back seats, and taxis are licensed to carry up to four people. The **Taxi Complaints Hotline** (☎ 1800 648 478 in Australia) deals with problem taxi drivers. The main cab companies are **Taxis Combined** (☎ 13 33 00); **RSL Taxis** (☎ 02/9581 1111); **Legion Cabs** (☎ 13 14 51); and **Premier Cabs** (☎ 13 10 17).

# Fast **Facts**

ATMS/CASHPOINTS  ATMs are everywhere and most use global networks such as Cirrus and PLUS. Australian ATMs use a four-digit code, so check with your bank and make sure you change yours before you leave home. Many banks impose a fee every time you use a card at another bank's ATM, and that fee can be higher for international transactions ($5 or more) than for domestic ones.

BABYSITTING  **Dial-an-Angel** (☎ 02/9416 7511; www.dialan angel.com) is a well-regarded babysitting service. Many high-end hotels also offer a babysitting service.

B&BS  The **Bed & Breakfast and Farmstay Accommodation Directory** (☎ 1300 888 862; www.bedandbreakfastnsw.com) is the best place to go to find B&Bs in and around Sydney.

BANKING HOURS  Banks are open Monday to Friday 9am to 5pm, and some, especially in the city center, are open Saturday 9:30am to 12:30pm.

BIKE RENTALS  Things are slowly getting better thanks to a bike-friendly mayor, but on the whole, Sydney is still not a particularly bike-friendly city, although Centennial Park has a great cycle track and there is a dedicated cycle path from the park to Bondi Beach. Rent bikes

from **Centennial Park Cycles** (50 Clovelly Rd., Randwick; ☎ 02/9398 5027; www.cyclehire.com.au).

BUSINESS & SHOP HOURS  Shopping hours are usually from 8:30am to 5:30pm daily (9am–5pm Sat), and most shops stay open until 9pm on Thursday. Most are open from around 10am to 4pm on Sunday.

CLIMATE  See "The Weather," earlier in this chapter.

CONSULATES & EMBASSIES  All foreign embassies are based in Canberra. You'll find the following consulates in Sydney: **Canada,** Level 5, 111 Harrington St., The Rocks (☎ 02/9364 3000); **New Zealand,** 55 Hunter St. (☎ 1300 559 535); **U.K.,** Level 16, Gateway Building, 1 Macquarie Place, Circular Quay (☎ 02/9247 7521); **U.S.,** Level 59, MLC Centre, 19–29 Martin Place (☎ 02/9373 9200).

CREDIT CARDS  Visa and MasterCard are universally accepted in Australia; American Express and Diners Club are less common and both usually attract a surcharge; Discover is not used. Always carry a little cash, because many merchants will not take cards for purchases under $15.

CUSTOMS  The duty-free allowance in Australia is $900 (under-18s, $450). "Dutiable goods" are luxury items such as perfume, watches, jewelry, furs, plus gifts of any kind.

Anyone over 18 can bring in up to 250 cigarettes or 250 grams of cigars or other tobacco products, and 2.25 liters (41 fluid oz.) of alcohol. Because Australia is an island, it is free of many agricultural and livestock diseases. To keep it that way, **strict quarantine** applies to importing plants, animals, and their products, including food. Sniffer dogs detect these products (as well as drugs) at airports. Amnesty bins are available before you reach the immigration counters in airport arrivals halls for items such as fruit. Don't be alarmed if, just before landing, the flight attendants spray the aircraft cabin (with products approved by the World Health Organization) to kill disease-bearing insects. For more information on what is and is not allowed, contact the **Australian Quarantine and Inspection Service** (☎ 02/6272 3933; www.daff.gov.au/aqis). The website www.customs.gov.au has a list of restricted or banned foods, animal and plant products, and other items.

**DENTISTS**  See "Emergencies," below.

**DOCTORS**  See "Emergencies," below.

**ELECTRICITY**  The current is 240 volts AC, 50 hertz. Sockets take two or three flat prongs. International visitors will need an adapter (best bought at home as most Australian shops only stock adapters for Australian appliances to fit international outlets). Power does not start automatically when you plug in an appliance; you need to flick the switch beside the socket, and turn it off before pulling the plug.

**EMBASSIES**  See "Consulates & Embassies," above.

**EMERGENCIES**  Dial ☎ **000** to call the police, the fire service, or an ambulance. Ask the concierge at your hotel to direct you to a doctor or dentist, or go online to www.health.nsw.gov.au. The **NRMA** will help if your car breaks down (☎ 13 11 11). If you are not a member of an auto club at home that has a reciprocal agreement with the NRMA, you'll have to join on the spot before they will tow or repair your car. This usually costs around $155, but is valid for 12 months.

**EVENT LISTINGS**  Good sources of event and entertainment listings include **Time Out magazine**, the Metro section of Friday's **Sydney Morning Herald**, and the entertainment and arts sections of the weekend newspapers. The free street press publications, **Brag** and **Drum Media,** are good for live music.

**FAMILY TRAVEL**  To locate accommodations, restaurants, and attractions that are particularly kid-friendly, refer to the Kids icon throughout this guide. Most Sydney hotels accommodate families; all but the most expensive restaurants are kid-friendly, although not all offer specific children's menus.

**GAY & LESBIAN TRAVELERS**  Sydney is one of the most gay-friendly cities in the world; the gay community has a high profile and lots of support services. There are plenty of gay and lesbian bars, particularly in Oxford Street in Darlinghurst and in Newtown, although overt demonstrations of gay affection are not always tolerated on the street. The annual Gay and Lesbian Mardi Gras festival and parade in February is one of the biggest events of the year. The **Gay and Lesbian Counselling Line** (☎ 02/8594 9596) is open 5:30pm to 10:30pm daily.

**HOLIDAYS**  Almost everything is closed on December 25 (Christmas Day) and Good Friday. On all other major public holidays—January 1 (New Year's Day), January 26 (Australia Day), Easter Sunday, Easter Monday, April 25 (Anzac Day), the second Monday in June (Queen's Birthday), the first Monday in October (Labour

The Savvy Traveler

Day), and December 26 (Boxing Day)—banks and businesses are closed, but larger shops and some tourist attractions may remain open.

INSURANCE Check your existing insurance policies before you buy travel insurance to cover trip cancellation, lost luggage, medical expenses, or car rental insurance. Australia has Reciprocal Health Care Agreements (RHCA) operating with Finland, Italy, Malta, New Zealand, Norway, Republic of Ireland, Sweden, The Netherlands, and the U.K., which allows restricted access to health care services. See www.medicareaustralia.gov.au.

INTERNET CAFES There's no shortage of Internet cafes and e-mail centers in Sydney, and you'll find many clustered around Central Station, Kings Cross, Bondi, and Manly. Many cafes and hotels also offer free wireless for paying customers. Public libraries also offer Internet access.

LOST PROPERTY Call credit card companies the minute you discover your wallet has been lost or stolen and file a report at the nearest police station. Your credit card company or insurer may require a police report number or record. For items lost on trains, contact the **Lost Property Office,** opposite platform 1 at Central Railway Station (☎ 02/9379 3341). The office is open Monday to Friday 8am to 5pm. For items left behind on planes or at the airport, go to the Federal Airport Corporation's administration office on the top floor of the International Terminal at Sydney International Airport (☎ 02/9667 9583). For stuff left behind on buses or ferries, call ☎ 131 500. Each taxi company also has its own lost property office.

MAIL & POSTAGE Stamps for standard-size mail inside Australia are 60¢; to send a postcard outside Australia will cost $1.60 and will usually take between 3 and 10 working days to reach the destination. Stamps are only available from post offices, although you can post a stamped letter or postcard at any red post box around the city. The **General Post Office (GPO)** is at 130 Pitt St., near Martin Place (☎ 13 13 18; Mon–Fri 8:30am–5:30pm, Sat 10am–2pm). General-delivery letters can be sent c/o Poste Restante, GPO, Sydney, NSW 2000, Australia (☎ 02/9244 3733), and collected at 310 George St., on the third floor of the Hunter Connection shopping center. It's open Monday to Friday 8:15am to 5:30pm.

MONEY The Australian dollar is divided into 100¢. Coins are 5¢, 10¢, 20¢, and 50¢ pieces (silver) and $1 and $2 pieces (gold). Even though prices often end in a variant of 1¢ and 2¢ (for example, 68¢ or $1.99), prices are rounded to the nearest 5¢—so 97¢ rounds down to 95¢, and 58¢ rounds up to 60¢. Bank notes come in denominations of $5, $10, $20, $50, and $100. Most major bank branches offer currency exchange services. Small foreign-currency exchange offices are clustered at the airport and around Circular Quay and Kings Cross. Most larger shops will accept traveler's checks, but they may be hard to cash at smaller shops and restaurants, so ask first.

OPTICIANS Eyeglasses can be repaired and contact lenses purchased at any optometrist in the city; take your prescription with you.

PARKING There is virtually no free parking in the city center; parking meter rates vary depending on the time and location. All meters accept coins and some will accept credit cards or payment via your mobile phone. Peak hours are 8am to 6pm and off-peak hours are 6 to 10pm. City Rangers keep an eagle eye on the few metered spots and will issue a fine to anyone who parks over time or illegally and the minimum fine is around $88. Many hotels offer parking, but at a fee—expect to pay upward of $25 per day. There are a number of parking stations throughout the city center and most offer good early-bird rates for full-day weekday parking if you enter 6:30am to 9:30am and exit 3:30pm to 7:30pm ($20–$30). Otherwise, expect to pay around $15 to $25 per hour; rates are much cheaper on weekends and evenings.

**PASSES** The **See Sydney Card** gives free entry to more than 40 attractions. You can visit as many of the attractions as you want and may also visit the same attraction more than once on different days, although to really gain value you'd need to visit a lot of attractions. Adult and kids cards are available, with or without transport, for 2, 3, and 7 days. Prices range from $155 to $339 adults; $110 to $220 kids. Order at www.seesydneycard.com.

**PASSPORTS & VISAS** Along with a current passport valid for the length of your stay, the Australian government requires a visa from visitors of every nation to be issued before you arrive (except New Zealand). Short-term tourist and business visas (up to 3 months) are issued instantly online, and called an **Electronic Travel Authority (ETA).** This is an electronic visa that takes the place of a stamp in your passport and is electronically recorded on Australian government systems. To apply online, visit www.eta.immi. gov.au; the $20 charge is payable by credit card. Applications for ETAs can also be submitted through travel agents or airlines. Apply for non-ETA visas at Australian embassies, consulates, and high commissions. See www.immi.gov.au for more information.

**PHARMACIES** Most often called "chemists," most suburbs have at least one pharmacy that is open late. You can also buy over-the-counter medications, such as headache tablets and cough syrups, at supermarkets. Australian pharmacists may only fill prescriptions written by Australian doctors, so carry enough medication with you for your trip.

**POLICE** Dial ☎ 000 for police.

**SAFETY** Sydney is a safe city, but just like any big city, it pays to be careful and use common sense. Keep your wallet hidden, don't wear money belts, bum packs, or fanny packs outside your clothing. Areas in which to be careful, especially at night, include Kings Cross, Redfern, around Central Station, the cinema strip on George Street near Town Hall station, and the southern end of King Street in Newtown. Inner city back lanes should also be avoided. The eastern beach suburbs of Bondi and Coogee can also be rough after midnight and the early hours of the morning when pubs and clubs close. If traveling by train at night (not recommended for solo women), travel in the carriages next to the guard's van, marked with a blue light on the outside. For most visitors, the most dangerous thing they encounter in Sydney is the surf: Always swim or surf at patrolled beaches between the red and yellow flags that mark the safest area for swimming.

**SENIOR TRAVELERS** Visiting seniors (often called "pensioners" in Australia) from other countries don't automatically qualify for the discounted entry prices to tours, attractions, transport, and events that Australian seniors enjoy, but it is always worth asking. Carry ID that shows your age.

**SMOKING** Smoking is banned in all enclosed public places, including public transport, offices, hospitals, hotels, bars, and restaurants. Some hotels have outdoor sections where smoking is permitted, often called "beer gardens." It is illegal to smoke in cars carrying children 15 and under.

TAXES   Australia imposes a 10% **goods and services tax (GST)** on most goods sold in Australia and most services. The GST applies to most travel-related goods and services, including transport, hotels, tours, and restaurants. By law, the tax has to be included in the advertised price of the product, though it doesn't have to be displayed independently of the pretax price. The **Tourist Refund Scheme (TRS)** enables you to claim a refund of the GST and 29% **wine equalization tax (WET)** paid on purchases of more than $300 (GST inclusive) in the one shop (as long as they are all on the one tax invoice) in the 30 days before you leave the country. You must wear or carry the goods on board the aircraft or ship and present them along with your original tax invoice, passport, and international boarding pass to a Customs officer at a TRS facility at the international airport or cruise terminal. A departure tax (officially called a Passenger Movement Charge) of $47 is payable by all persons 12 years or older upon leaving Australia, and it is generally included in the airline or cruise ticket price.

TAXIS   See "Getting Around," earlier in this chapter.

TELEPHONES   Sydney's public phone boxes, when they are in working order, take coins. Many also accept credit cards and $10 phone cards available from newsdealers. **Local calls** cost 50¢, no matter how long you talk, but don't return unused coins (you won't get any change back if you use a $2 coin to pay for a 50¢ local call). Numbers beginning with 1800 within Australia

are toll-free; numbers starting with 13 or 1300 in Australia are charged at the local fee; numbers beginning with 1900 (or 1901 or 1902, and so on) are pay-for-service lines, and you will be charged as much as $5 per minute. To make **international calls** from Australia: First dial 0011 and then the country code (U.S. or Canada: 1; U.K.: 44; Ireland: 353; New Zealand: 64), then the area code and number. For **directory assistance:** Dial ☎ 12455 for a number inside Australia, and ☎ 1225 for numbers to all other countries. The international calling code for Australia is 61.

TIPPING   Tipping is not expected anywhere, but certainly appreciated. Most Australians leave tips for good restaurant service, but usually only in expensive restaurants. The usual amount is 10%, with more for exemplary service. Tips are often pooled and shared among all staff. In hotels, if you want to tip luggage porters, $1 to $2 is plenty, as is a small gratuity of $2 to $5 for those who deliver room service, but no more than 10% of the bill. Most people also tip taxi drivers any small change left over from the fare and $5 to $10 for tour guides.

TOURIST OFFICES   The **Sydney Visitor Centre at The Rocks** is a good place to pick up maps, brochures, and general tourist information about Sydney as well as towns in New South Wales (first floor, The Rocks Centre, corner Argyle and Playfair sts., The Rocks; ☎ 02/9240 8788; www.sydneyvisitorcenter. com; daily 9am–5pm). There's also the **Sydney Visitors Centre Darling Harbour** (33 Wheat Rd., Darling Harbour, near the IMAX Theatre; daily 9:30am–5:30pm). The **Manly Visitors Information Centre** is at Manly Wharf (☎ 02/9976 1430; Mon–Fri 9am–5pm, weekends 10am–4pm).

**TOURIST TRAPS** Overall, Sydney is a tourist-friendly city. As a general rule, avoid restaurants that have a waiter outside vying for your business—and you're pretty much guaranteed not to get good value Aboriginal art at any souvenir shop. The main scam to look out for is at busy taxi queues, when drivers may try to cash in by insisting you share a cab with other passengers in line at the airport. After dropping off the other passengers, the cabdriver will attempt to charge you the full price of the journey, despite the fact that the other passengers paid for their sections, and you will have had a longer than normal ride in the process. If you are first in line in the taxi stand, the law states that you can refuse to share the cab.

**TOURS   Sydney Visitors Centre** (see "Tourist Offices," above) is the best place to go for information (and bookings) about tours in and around Sydney. Recommended are the Sydney and Bondi Explorer buses (see "Getting Around," earlier in this chapter), and **AAT Kings,** who offer a number of sightseeing bus tours in and around the city (☎ 02/9028 5182; www.aatkings.com).

**TRAVELERS WITH DISABILITIES** Most hotels, major stores, attractions, and public toilets in Australia have wheelchair access, although the entrance or access may not be obvious and it may pay to call ahead. Some (but not all) buses and taxis (it's a good idea to book 24 hr. in advance for taxis) have wheelchair access facilities, but many suburban train stations outside the city center have stair access only. You can check access facilities at www.131500.com.au, or call ☎ 131 500. Holders of vision impaired persons' passes are entitled to free travel on CityRail, Sydney Buses, and Sydney Ferries. Guide dogs and hearing assistance animals are permitted on these services and in all shops and restaurants. If you wish to visit Australia with your guide dog, remember that animals must satisfy certain health requirements and may need to undergo quarantine after arrival (visit www.daff.gov.au for more information). TTY facilities are still limited largely to government services.

**WEATHER**   For the local forecast, call ☎ 1196 or visit www.bom.gov.au.

# Sydney: **A Brief History**

**4000 B.C.–A.D. 1780** The area around present-day Sydney is home to around 3,000 Aborigines—the Eora people, made up of various clans.

**1770** English explorer James Cook arrives at Botany Bay.

**1778** Penal Colony of New South Wales established by the arrival of the first fleet of 11 convict ships under Governor Arthur Philip. Days later, French

explorer Comte de La Pérouse arrives in Botany Bay. Sydney is named after Thomas Townshend, 1st Viscount Sydney, who was the British home secretary at the time, and the man responsible for the planned convict colony in Australia.

**1790** Colony faces starvation as few of the convicts know how to farm, particularly in the reversed Southern Hemisphere seasons.

The arrival of second fleet of convicts does little to alleviate food shortages.

1791 Arrival of third fleet. Colony remains close to starvation until 1795, when the first successful farms are established by free convicts.

1793 The first free settlers arrive.

1803 Sydney's first newspaper, the *Sydney Gazette* is published.

1808 Governor William Bligh, of mutiny on the *Bounty* fame, is ousted by the NSW Corps in the Rum Rebellion—the only successful armed takeover of government in Australia's recorded history.

1809 The first post office in Australia opens on George Street.

1813 The Blue Mountains are crossed by explorers Wentworth, Blaxland, and Lawson, opening up the western plains to settlement.

1831 *Sydney Morning Herald* is published.

1842 Sydney becomes a city.

1847 Convict population of Sydney accounts for just 3.2% of the total population.

1850 Due to pressure from the citizens of Sydney, England stops transport of convicts to NSW. Sydney University founded.

1851 The discovery of gold in Bathurst sparks a massive influx of people from all over the world seeking their fortunes.

1871 Population of Sydney tops 200,000.

1888 Town Hall opens.

1900 Outbreak of bubonic plague in The Rocks kills 103 people. Large-scale slum clearances result.

1901 Australia becomes part of the Commonwealth.

1925 Population of Sydney reaches 1,000,000.

1926 The first part of the underground railway system opens.

1932 Sydney Harbour Bridge opens.

1942 Three Japanese midget submarines enter Sydney Harbour. One of them fires the torpedo that hits HMAS *Kuttabul,* killing 21.

1973 The Sydney Opera House is completed.

1978 First gay Mardi Gras is held as a protest march; 53 of the marchers are arrested.

1981 Sydney Tower built.

1988 Aborigines demonstrate as Australia celebrates its bicentenary with a reenactment of the arrival of the First Fleet's entry into Sydney Harbour.

1992 Sydney Harbour Tunnel built.

2000 Sydney is host to the Olympic Games.

2006 Population of Sydney hits 4.28 million.

2007 Sydney Opera House is included on the UNESCO World Heritage List.

2008 Pope Benedict XVI is welcomed by a crowd of 500,000 during World Youth Day celebrations—the largest in Australian history.

2011 City of Sydney becomes first carbon-neutral council in Australia.

2012 Work begins on one of the city's biggest urban renewal projects, Barangaroo, at the old dockyards on the eastern side of Darling Harbour.

# Toll-Free Numbers & Websites

**Airlines**

**AIR CALIN**
☎ 1300 364 181
www.aircalin.nc

**AIR CANADA**
☎ 1300 655 767 www.aircanada.com

**AIR CHINA**
☎ 02/9232-7277
www.airchina.com.cn

**AIR FRANCE**
☎ 1300 390 190
www.airfrance.com

**AIR MAURITIUS**
☎ 1300 658 572
www.airmauritius.com

**AIR NEW ZEALAND**
☎ 13 24 76
www.airnewzealand.com

**AIR NIUGINI**
☎ 1300 361 380
www.airniugini.com.pg

**AIR PACIFIC**
☎ 1 800 230 150
www.airpacific.com

**AIR TAHITI NUI**
☎ 1300 732 415
www.airtahitinui.com.au

**AIR VANUATU**
☎ 1300 780 737
www.airvanuatu.com

**ASIANA AIRLINES**
☎ 1300 767 234
www.flyasiana.com

**BRITISH AIRWAYS**
☎ 1300 767 177
www.britishairways.com

**CATHAY PACIFIC**
☎ 13 17 47
www.cathaypacific.com

**CHINA AIRLINES**
☎ 02/9231 5588
www.china-airlines.com

**CHINA EASTERN**
☎ 02/9290 1148
www.flychinaeastern.com

**CHINA SOUTHERN**
☎ 02/9233 9788
www.flychinasouthern.com

**EMIRATES**
☎ 1300 303 777
www.emirates.com

**ETIHAD AIRWAYS**
☎ 1800 998 995
www.etihadairways.com

**GARUDA INDONESIA**
☎ 1300 365 330
www.garuda-indonesia.com

**HAWAIIAN AIRLINES**
☎ 1300 669 106
www.hawaiianairlines.com.au

**JAPAN AIRLINES**
☎ 1300 525 287
www.jal.com

**JETSTAR**
☎ 13 15 38
www.jetstar.com

**KOREAN AIR**
☎ 02/9262 6000
www.koreanair.com

**LANCHILE**
☎ 02/9244 2333
www.lan.com

**MALAYSIA AIRLINES**
☎ 13 26 27
www.malaysiaairlines.com

**PACIFIC BLUE**
☎ 13 16 45
www.flypacificblue.com

**PHILIPPINE AIRLINES**
☎ 1 300 888 725
www.philippineairlines.com

**POLYNESIAN BLUE**
☎ 13 16 45
www.polynesianblue.com

**QANTAS**
☎ 13 13 13
www.qantas.com.au

**REX—REGIONAL EXPRESS**
☎ 13 17 13
www.regionalexpress.com.au

**ROYAL BRUNEI AIRLINES**
☎ 1300 721 271
www.bruneiair.com

**SINGAPORE AIRLINES**
☎ 13 10 11
www.singaporeair.com

**SOUTH AFRICAN AIRWAYS**
☎ 1300 435 972
www.flysaa.com

**THAI AIRWAYS**
☎ 1300 651 960
www.thaiair.com

**UNITED AIRLINES**
☎ 13 17 77
www.united.com

**V AUSTRALIA**
☎ 13 82 87
www.vaustralia.com.au

**VIETNAM AIRLINES**
☎ 1300 888 028
www.vietnamairlines.com.vn

**VIRGIN ATLANTIC**
☎ 1300 727 340
www.virgin-atlantic.com

**VIRGIN AUSTRALIA**
☎ 13 67 89
www.virginaustralia.com

## Car Rental Agencies

**AVIS**
☎ 13 63 33
www.avis.com

**BAYSWATER**
☎ 02/9360 3622
www.bayswatercarrental.com.au

**BUDGET**
☎ 1300 362 848
www.budget.com.au

**EUROPCAR**
☎ 1300 131 390
www.europcar.com.au

**HERTZ**
☎ 13 30 39
www.hertz.com.au

**THRIFTY**
☎ 1300 367 227
www.thrifty.com.au

# Index

See also Accommodations and Restaurant indexes, below.

# Photo **Credits**

viii: © Anthony Anderton; p 4, bottom: © Anthony Anderton; p 5, top: © Anthony Anderton; p 5, bottom: © Anthony Anderton; p 6, top: Courtesy Shark Dive Extreme, Oceanworld Manly, Sydney Australia; p 6, bottom: © Anthony Anderton; p 7: © Anthony Anderton; p 9, bottom: © Anthony Anderton; p 10, top: © Lee Atkinson; p 10, bottom: © Anthony Anderton; p 11, top: © Anthony Anderton; p 15, top: © Anthony Anderton; p 15, bottom: © Anthony Anderton; p 16, top: © Anthony Anderton; p 16, bottom: © Anthony Anderton; p 17, top: Photo by Dan Boud, Courtesy Sydney Opera House Trust; p 19, bottom: © Anthony Anderton; p 20, top: © Anthony Anderton; p 21: © Anthony Anderton; p 23, bottom: © Anthony Anderton; p 24, bottom: © Anthony Anderton; p 25, top: © Anthony Anderton; p 27, bottom: © Anthony Anderton; p 28, bottom: © Anthony Anderton; p 29, top: © Anthony Anderton; p 29, bottom: © Anthony Anderton; p 31, top: © Lee Atkinson; p 31, bottom: © Anthony Anderton; p 32, top: © Anthony Anderton; p 32, bottom: © Anthony Anderton; p 33, top: © Anthony Anderton; p 33, bottom: © Anthony Anderton; p 35, bottom: © Lee Atkinson; p 36, top: © Anthony Anderton; p 37, top: © Anthony Anderton; p 37, bottom: © Anthony Anderton; p 39, bottom: © Anthony Anderton; p 40, top: © Anthony Anderton; p 40, bottom: © Anthony Anderton; p 41, top: © Lee Atkinson; p 44, top: © Lee Atkinson; p 44, bottom: © Anthony Anderton; p 45, top: © Anthony Anderton; p 45, bottom: Photo by Greg Barrett, Courtesy Bangarra Dance Theatre; p 47, top: © Anthony Anderton; p 49, top: © Anthony Anderton; p 49, bottom: © Anthony Anderton; p 50, top: © Lee Atkinson; p 51: © Anthony Anderton; p 53, top: © Anthony Anderton; p 54, bottom: © Anthony Anderton; p 55, top: © Anthony Anderton; p 57, top: © Anthony Anderton; p 58, bottom: © Anthony Anderton; p 59, top: © Anthony Anderton; p 60, bottom: © Anthony Anderton; p 61, top: © Lee Atkinson; p 61, bottom: © Anthony Anderton; p 63, top: © Lee Atkinson; p 64, bottom: © Lee Atkinson; p 65: © Anthony Anderton; p 66, bottom: © Lee Atkinson; p 71, top: © Anthony Anderton; p 72, top: © Anthony Anderton; p 72, bottom: © Anthony Anderton; p 73, top: © Anthony Anderton; p 73, bottom: © Anthony Anderton; p 74, top: © Anthony Anderton; p 75, bottom: © Anthony Anderton; p 76, top: © Anthony Anderton; p 77: © Anthony Anderton; p 80, top: © Anthony Anderton; p 81, top: © Anthony Anderton; p 81, bottom: © Anthony Anderton; p 83, top: © Ben Lewis/Alamy ; p 84, bottom: © Don Fuchs/LOOK Die Bildagentur der Fotografen GmbH/Alamy ; p 85, top: © Anthony Anderton; p 85, bottom: © Anthony Anderton; p 87, bottom: © Anthony Anderton; p 88, bottom: © Anthony Anderton; p 89: © Anthony Anderton; p 96, bottom: © Anthony Anderton; p 97, top: Courtesy Café Sydney; p 98, top: © Anthony Anderton; p 98, bottom: © Anthony Anderton; p 99, top: Courtesy Hilton Sydney; p 100, bottom: © Anthony Anderton; p 102, top: © Anthony Anderton; p 102, bottom: © Anthony Anderton; p 103, bottom: © Anthony Anderton; p 104, top: © Anthony Anderton; p 105: © Anthony Anderton; p 106, bottom: Courtesy Merivale; p 112, top: Courtesy Shangri-La Hotels & Resorts; p 113, top: Courtesy Marble Bar at Hilton Sydney; p 113, bottom: © Anthony Anderton; p 114, top: Courtesy The Victoria Room; p 115, bottom: © Anthony Anderton; p 116, middle: © Andrew Watson/John Warburton-Lee Photography/Alamy; p 117, bottom: © Anthony Anderton; p 118, top: © Anthony Anderton; p 118, bottom: Courtesy The Vanguard; p 119: © Anthony Anderton; p 126, bottom: © Anthony Anderton; p 127, top: © Anthony Anderton; p 127, bottom: Photo by Prudence Upton, Courtesy Sydney Opera House Trust; p 128, bottom: © Anthony Anderton; p 130, top: Photo by Tony Mott, Courtesy Big Day Out; p 131: Courtesy Blue Sydney, A Taj Hotel; p 132, bottom: Courtesy Shangri-La Hotels & Resorts; p 136, bottom: Courtesy The Star; p 139, bottom: Courtesy Observatory Hotel/LHW; p 140, top: Courtesy Shangri-La Hotels & Resorts; p 141, bottom: Courtesy YHA, Ltd.; p 142, top: Courtesy Taj Hotels Resorts And Palaces; p 143: © Anthony Anderton; p 145, bottom: © Anthony Anderton; p 146, bottom: © Ashley Cooper/Alamy; p 147, bottom: © Aileen Mayer/Frommers.com Community; p 149, top: © Anthony Anderton; p 150, bottom: © Roche Group Hunter Valley Gardens; p 151, top: Courtesy Balloon Aloft; p 153, top: © Anthony Anderton; p 154, top: © Anthony Anderton; p 155, top: © Anthony Anderton; p 155, bottom: © Anthony Anderton; p 157, top: © Anthony Anderton; p 157, bottom: Courtesy Australia Reptile Park; p 158, top: Courtesy Firescreek Fruit Winery; p 158, bottom: Courtesy Cardno Ecology Lab; p 159, top: © Anthony Anderton; p 160, top: © Anthony Anderton; p 161: © Anthony Anderton

# Notes